Models and Paradig n
Science an

By : Mung, Gin Lian

TABLE OF CONTENTS

CHAPTER ONE

GALILEO'S GOD OF REASON

CHAPTER ONE

GALILEO'S GOD OF REASON

Introduction

The fundamental concern of both science and religion is to make some sort of sense of life, to discern some sort of order in the world. Yet, in the past, they were exaggerated claims as constantly at intellectual conflict and completely at odds by various thinkers. From the scientific point of view, religion is not empirically based and is therefore irrelevant to science. From the theological point of view, science is not based on Divine revelation, and is therefore irrelevant to religion. Even today this compartmentalized view is not uncommon in popular and professional circles.

However, pioneer modern scientists and natural philosophers were good at practising religion and found no real incompatibility between their life as a scientist and as a believer. Far from any cognitive enmity between science and religion, Divine Will and Reason were fundamental for natural philosophers because on it was based their understanding of the universe and the laws governing it. The founders of modern science expected to find 'law' in nature because they believed in a Lawgiver.

In this chapter, I will begin with rationalist components of Galileo's conception of natural science. He held that God had created the world and the laws of nature according to His reason, and that human reason is capable of discerning the nature of that creation. I have argued that Galileo's approach to the laws of nature, has a strongly rational character. From this characteristic of nature there follows the necessity of natural laws, which Galileo believes can be established with certainty. In doing so he maintained that the truths of mathematics possess an absolute nature that is independent of God.

Like other natural philosophers of the seventeenth century, Galileo held that nature was an orderly system, and mathematical in character. By this he meant that it was mathematics, and especially geometry, which gave us the key to the understanding of the physical universe. Galileo held that nature is "inexorable and immutable and never passes the laws imposed upon her."[1] The human mind could comprehend those laws and the failure to fathom the depths of nature is due to the fact that man is a created being with a finite mind. Galileo's ideal of scientific knowledge was that of mathematical demonstration, which he believed to be the only way in which we describe nature. Galileo's ideal of a science of nature was grounded on a

---

[1] Galileo Galilei, *Letters on the Sunspots*, translated by Still Drake (New York: Doubleday Anchor Books, 1957), p. 136.

rationalistic understanding of God's relation to created objects and minds.

Galileo's Theology of Creation

Giorgio Spini's remark that apart from his letter to the Grand Duchess Christiana, which was hardly a spontaneous assertion of deep religious conviction, Galileo never wrote on any theological subject – which understates the case.[2] As a matter of fact, Galileo did write on creation. Galileo made enough theological statements for us to assemble a picture of his theology of creation. Scholars, who held persistently to the positivist picture of Galileo, refused to allow that Galileo ever engaged in metaphysical speculation.[3] Maurice Clavelin, I think, comes much closer to the truth. To hold that

"Mathematical reason is capable of embracing reality, to assume that rational necessity is akin to natural necessity, to turn simplicity into a touchstone of scientific explanation is not to introduce ostensive definitions based on the evidence of our senses, but rather to choose a metaphysical position."[4]

---

[2] Galileo Galilei, "Letter to the Princess Christina" in *The Galileo Affair: A Documentary History*, edited and translated by Maurice A. Finocchiaro (Berkeley: University of California Press, 1989), p. 108.

[3] Edward W. Strong, *Galileo: Man of Science* (New York: Basil Books, 1967), p. 352.

[4] Jerome J. Langford, *Galileo, Science, and the Church* (Berkeley: University of California Press, 1978), p. 10.

Certainly Galileo did so consciously in the *Dialogue Concerning the Two Chief World Systems,*[5] where the debate between Salviati and Simplicio hinged on the relevance of mathematics to the physical world.[6] Galileo's assumption concerning nature, the core of his philosophy of science is explained thus:

"Philosophy is written in this grand book – I mean the universe –which stands continually open to our gaze, but it cannot be understood unless one first learns to comprehend the language and interpret the characters in which it is written. It is written in the language of mathematics, and its characters are triangles, circles, and other geometrical figures, without which it is humanly impossible to understand a single word of it; without these, one is wandering about in a dark labyrinth.[7]

---

[5] G. Galileo, *Dialogue Concerning the Two Chief World Systems*, translated by Stillman Drake (Berkeley: University of California Press, 1953), p.14. Galileo choose to cast his argument for Copernicanism in the form of a discussion between three interlocutors. The first two, the Florentine Filippo Salviati and the Venetian Patrican Giovanfrancesco Sagredo, had been his friends; the third, the Aristotelian Simplicio, was an imaginary character. They are presented as having gathered in Sagredo's palace at Venice for four days to discuss the arguments for and against the heliocentric system. Salviati is a militant Copernican, Simplicio an avowed defender of geocentrism, and Sagredo an intelligent amateur already half converted to the new astronomy.

[6] Aristotelian Simplicio maintained that in physical and natural matters one need not always require a mathematical demonstration Simplicio did not come over to Salviati's position until the First Day of the Dialogue, when he admitted that "if I were to begin my studies over again, I should try to follow the advice of Plato and commence from mathematics, which proceeds so carefully, and does not admit as certain anything except what it has conclusively proved." On the Second Day he added, "truly, I begin to understand that although logic is a very excellent instrument to govern our reasoning, it does not compare with the sharpness of geometry in awakening the mind to discovery or invention."

[7] Drake, 1953, pp. 151-336. Galileo restated the Pythagorean-Platonic standpoint in his own words by proclaiming that the book of nature is a book written by God in the language of mathematics.

The Platonic flavor of such passage has presented credence to the notion that Galileo can be understood as a Platonist. He himself emphasized on pure reason and mathematics as over and against Aristotelian's reliance on direct sense experience. But Plato's concept of God differed from Galileo's, and consequently so did his conception of science. Although Plato's Demiurge had wanted to make a perfect world, matter had limited him. Plato's concept of "Reason" had not been wholly successful, so the product was only an imperfect copy of the ideal reality. Physical things did not perfectly embody the mathematical forms of the world of being which alone were fully comprehensible. Physics, the study of physical objects, could not be a true science capable of giving knowledge.

On the other hand, for Galileo, being the work of the omnipotent God, the world is most perfect. And Galileo added that as such it is of necessity most orderly, having its parts disposed in the highest and perfect order among themselves. The "Book of Nature" which Galileo was intending to read, which he believed is written in the language of mathematics, is not a book of the Platonic kind. According to Galileo, God created the universe by using mathematical archetypes, and hence every part of the universe has been created in accordance with mathematical principles and rules.[8] Epistemologically, this principle stated that what is mathematical is rational: mathematics is the key to understanding the laws of nature. Galileo's interest is to define natural phenomena in analogous terms with mathematical objects. His attempt is to apply mathematics in the world of natural phenomena.

It was the traditional Aristotelian cosmology and physics which Galileo set up as the chief opponent. According to Aristotle, circular motion was primarily the most perfect motion: circular motion is necessarily primary. By perfect motion he meant a continuous motion, one without terminus, since a motion, which began and ended at discrete points would be incomplete and imperfect. Circular motion since it is eternal and perfectly continuous, lacks terminus. Only the incomplete, the imperfect things move towards what they lack. The heavenly world was made up of ether, because of that their motion is perfect, so they move in a circular motion.

---

[8] Aristotelian philosophers of Galileo's day looked down on mathematicians and denigrated the study of mathematics as inferior—even irrelevant—to natural philosophy. Nature, in their view, could not be expected to follow precise numerical rules. But Galileo envisioned the experimental, mathematical analysis of Nature as the wave of the future. Among the first to bear out this prophecy was Isaac Newton, born within a year of Galileo's death, who codified mathematical laws of motion and universal gravitation. Posterity agrees that Galileo's great genius lay in his ability to observe the world at hand, to understand the behavior of its parts, and to describe these in terms of mathematical proportions. For these achievements, Albert Einstein named Galileo "the father of modern physics" —indeed of modern science altogether.

Accordingly the reason for believing in circularity is that the circle is a perfectly symmetric figure, rendering it most pleasing to the order. Religious reasons also dispelled any doubt concerning the universal validity of this principle in heavenly motion. The heavens were the abode of Divine beings. Nothing imperfect was admissible there. Since the circular motion alone was perfect motion, that alone could be allowed there. Of course in the geocentric system the marked deviation from circularity in the planetary path actually observed from the earth never went unnoticed.

However, astronomers did not allow these deviations to threaten this principle. It was stipulated that these irregularities should be treated as only apparent, to be accounted for in terms of regular circular motions. To us living in the twenty first century the arguments in favor of circularity look very unconvincing, to say the least. However, that was not the case in the days of Galileo, when Aristotle's authority still exerted a powerful influence, especially because no viable alternative physics was available at the time.

In contrast to Aristotelian's view on creation, Galileo had a positive and optimistic view toward the world. He believed that the material world is a reflection of the Divine. He questioned Aristotle's division of the universe into the terrestrial and celestial or the perfect and the imperfect. Galileo denied such distinction by observing that the heavenly bodies are like moon whose surface was not a smooth, perfect sphere, for, he observed the moon was marred with mountains and valleys, pits and craters. Galileo intuitively understood that the terrestrial spheres as well as the celestial sphere are made of the same constituent matter and both are capable of change.[9] This far reaching intuitive vision is expressed when Salviati, a spokesman of Galileo, argued that straight motion cannot exist in a well-ordered universe, if all integral bodies in the world are by nature movable, it is impossible that their motions should be straight, or anything else but circular.[10] The reason is that

"For whatever moves straight changes place, and continuing to move, goes farther from its starting point and from every place through which it successively passes. Only circular motion can preserves the cosmic order by keeping and moving the bodies in the same relative position and it follows that what does not naturally move in a circle must naturally be at rest. Besides, straight motion being by nature infinite (because a straight line is infinite and indeterminate), it is impossible that anything should have by nature moving in a straight line or, in other words, toward a place where it is impossible to arrive, there being no finite end. Only circular motion is suitable for a perfect world. God's perfect creative act was likewise the cause of circular motion in the celestial bodies."[11]

---

[9] When the Aristotelian Simplicio stated that the heavens are immutable because no change has ever been observed there, Salviati asks him how he can affirm that China and America are subject to change when he has only seen Europe.

[10] Galileo Galilei, "The Assayer," in *Discoveries and Opinion of Galileo*, translated by Still Drake (New York: Doubleday Anchor Books, 1957), p. 123.

[11] William Shea, *Galileo's Intellectual Revolution* (New York: Macmillan, 1972), p. 90.

Importantly in Galileo's thought is that God's perfect creation meant that His ideas had been realized in the objects He had created. Even the complexities of the movement of celestial circulations were subject to the scrutiny of geometry and can be expressed in mathematical terms. Simplicio, a true Aristotelian, argued that while mathematician Galileo might prove his propositions well enough in theory, things happened otherwise in practice when applied to sensible and physical matters. Galileo responded to Simplico that it would be novel if computations and ratios made in abstract numbers did not correspond to concrete gold and silver coins he received in return for his merchandise - and if they did not, he would be out of business. Surprisingly Galileo held that mathematical conclusions are the same in the concrete as they are in the abstract. Nevertheless, he recognized that in order this computation may apply precisely to concrete phenomena, a process of abstraction is mandatory.

"Just as the computer who wants his computations to deal with sugar, silk, and wool must discount the boxes, bales and other packings, so the mathematical scientist, when he wants to recognize in the concrete the effects he has proved in the abstract, must deduct the material hindrances, and if he is able to do so, I assure you that things are in no less agreement than arithmetical computations. The errors, then, lie not in the abstractness or concreteness, not in geometry or physics, but in a calculator who does not know how to make a true accounting."[12]

---

[12] Drake, 1957, p. 207.

Thus for Galileo, although nature might not be simple, it was nevertheless explicable in mathematical terms. There was "no intractable surd in the things of nature which defies rationalization."[13] Since the world was mathematical to the core, our failure to fathom the depths of the created order was attributed much more to the defect of a finite human understanding than to the exercise of Divine freedom. So much so the assumption of Galileo was that, since the Divine geometer had fully carried out His intentions, nature was at root mathematical, and amounted to the identification of mathematical form as the intelligible essence of celestial bodies. Galileo referred to the essences of bodies, not of substances, for he denied that we could know the true essences of substances in this world.[14] Nevertheless the essences of mathematical forms could in fact be known – properties could be deduced from definitions. In doing so to learn about a circle, we should begin with one of the simplest properties and taking this for the definition of a circle, proceed by reasoning to other properties.[15] God,

---

[13] Langford, p. 369.

[14] Ibid., p.145.

[15] In the *Assayer*, Galileo stated that regular lines are susceptible of definition and of having their qualities and properties. Thus the spinal is regular, and its definition originated in two uniform motions, one straight and the other circular; so is the ellipse, which originates from the cutting of a cone or a cylinder and so on. But irregular lines are those which have no determinacy whatever and are indefinite and casual, and hence indefinable. No property of such lines can be demonstrated, nor in a word can anything

who simply apprehends the circle's essences, knows without time-consuming reasoning all the infinity of its properties. To the degree that we, too, could know the essence of a form, to that same degree we could share in the Divine knowledge.

It is for this reason, Galileo indeed declared boldly that while man knows only a few of the mathematical truths perceived by God, his understanding of these few equals the Divine in objective certainty, for it succeeds in understanding necessity, beyond which there can be no greater certainty. To attain certitude, therefore, we must not depend on sense observation but on some kind of a priori knowledge (prior to sense experience) rooted in the human mind itself, presumably it had been implanted there by God, who has endowed us with reason and intellect.[16] Therefore, Galileo equated science with mathematics, a true and necessary demonstration. Probable arguments were not good enough; conclusions not proved by necessary demonstrations did not belong to science. Natural truths must follow necessarily, in such a way that it would be impossible for them to take place in any other manner, for, just as there is no middle ground

be known about them. Hence to say, 'such events take place by reason of an irregular line' is the same as saying, " I do not know why they occur." The introduction of such lines is in no way superior to the sympathy, antipathy, and other terms employed by some philosophers as a cloak for the correct reply, which would be: "I do not know."

[16] Drake, 1953, p. 90.

between truth and falsity in physical things, so in proofs one must either establish his point beyond any doubt or else beg the question.[17]

Galileo never assumed truth to have required proof. In Galileo's opinion, then, scientific conclusions ought to have the force of eternal conclusions.[18] But this would only be possible if God himself, as the Creator of the universe guaranteed that nature displayed the same characteristics as the mathematical language in which it was written, and further guaranteed that the human mind was capable of reading that language.[19] As far as I can tell Galilean philosophy, it is an attempt to establish that a natural kind – matter - possesses physical properties that can be understood mathematically.

As Galileo put it in *the Letter to the Grand Duchess*, he believed that nature is inexorable and immutable, and never passes the bounds of the laws assigned to her.[20] Unlike Plato, Galileo thought we could attain true

---

[17] Drake, 1957, p. 424.

[18] Ibid., p. 50. Galileo and Descartes held a common view of knowledge. But they differed on the role of mathematics in their respective systems. Descartes shunned a truly mathematical science for an essentially Aristotelian method of necessary demonstration from qualitative a priori principles, taking geometry as a paradigm of intelligibility but not in itself as a significant component of science. On the other hand, Galileo actually equated geometry with physical science.

[19] A favorite metaphor used in Galileo's days was to speak of nature as a book and God as the Author of that book, which is the focus of science.

[20] Drake, 1957, p. 182.

knowledge of material bodies. But he confessed that he was not far from being of the same opinion as Plato, who admired human understanding and believed it to partake of divinity simply because it understood the nature of numbers. Regardless of what one thinks, man was created in the image of God, this image consisted in man's rationality as somehow sharing in God's own rationality.

For Galileo human rationality was a mirror of Divine rationality. We are rational beings and human actions are governed by rational considerations. Although we, unlike God, are not omniscient, in certain limited cases human knowledge is as perfect as Divine. Thus, just as God is rational and is capable of knowing, we, too, are endowed with these capabilities. What the Divine intellect perceives in a flash, the mortal mind fits together bit by bit. Human mind is restricted in many respects, but it can attain certainty in the pure mathematical science alone; that is geometry and arithmetic, in which the Divine intellect indeed knows infinitely more proportions, since it knows all. But with regard to those few which the human intellect does understand, Galileo believed that its knowledge equals the Divine in objective certainty, for here it succeeds in understanding necessity, beyond which there can be no greater sureness.[21] Galileo goes to

[21] Drake, 1957, p. 103.

consider that such certainty was inborn. Presumably it had been implanted by God, who has endowed us with sense, reason and intellect. Certainly, Galileo did not want to say that humans were omniscient like God, such heretical views were far from him. However he did believe that God used mathematical archetypes and where these were involved, humans had access to God's knowledge.

Divine Transcendence and the Limits of Human Reason

According to British philosopher Michael B. Foster, "rationalism in theology is the doctrine that the activity of God is an activity of reason. It implies the corollary that the activity of reason in man, in so far as it is pure, is itself divine."[22] This, dominant theme of Galileo's theology, served as the foundation for Galileo's ideal of deductive science of necessary truths. Yet he did not lose sight of his limited capacity to participate in God's unlimited understanding of the creation. By means of the mathematical language, human knowledge can attain the truths that God knows, the only difference between human and Divine knowledge being the mode by which these truths

[22] Michael B. Foster, "Christian Theology and Modern Science of Nature," in *Mind* 45 (1936): 1.

are apprehended. Galileo pointed out that "the human understanding can be taken in two modes, the *intensive* or the *extensive*." Galileo contrasted God's extensive knowledge with the human's intensive knowledge. Intensively, man understands much; extensively, little. Intensively, with regard to understanding of the creation, Galileo said,

"The human intellect does understand some of them perfectly, and thus in these it has as much absolute certainty as Nature itself has. Of such are the mathematical sciences alone; that is, geometry, and arithmetic, in which the Divine intellect indeed knows infinitely more propositions, since it knows all. But with regard to those few which the human intellect does understand, I believe that its knowledge equals the Divine in objective certainty, for here it succeeds in understanding necessity, beyond which there can be no greater sureness."[23]

However, extensively, human understanding is nothing even if we understand a thousand propositions; for a thousand in relation to infinity is zero. God sees all the infinite cases. He knows all the infinite propositions in a way which is exceedingly more excellent than ours.

"Our method proceeds with reasoning by steps from one conclusion to another, while His is one of simple intuition. He illustrated that, for example, in order to acquire a knowledge of some property of the circle (which has an infinity of them), begin with one of the simplest, and, taking this for the definition of the circle, proceed by reasoning to another property, and from this to the third, and then a fourth, and so on. But the Divine intellect, by a simple apprehension of the circle's essence, knows without time consuming reasoning all the infinity of its properties. All these properties are in effect virtually included in the definitions of all things, and

[23] Drake, 1953, p. 103.

ultimately, through being infinite, are perhaps but one in their essence and in the Divine Mind."[24]

Whereas our intellect moves laboriously from one step to the next, the Divine mind moves like light in an instant;[25] which is the same as saying that everything is always present to it. The human mind was, according to Galileo, one the greatest of God's achievements. Certainly, in Galileo's eyes, mathematical demonstrations as such proved that human mind is the work of God and one of the most excellent works.

"*Our understanding, as well in the manner as in the number of things understood, is infinitely surpassed by the Divine; but I do not thereby abase it so much as to consider it absolutely null. No, when I consider what marvelous things and how many of them men have understood, inquired into, and contrived, I recognize and understand only too clearly that the human mind is a work of God's, and one of the most excellent."*[26]

Moreover Galileo rightly pointed out that our minds differ from God's both in kind and in degree. His knowledge of things is immediate and complete, ours only partial.[27] With respect to extensive and intensive understanding, Aristotelian Simplicio and Copernican Salviati were debating

---

[24] Drake, 1957, p. 104.

[25] Ibid., p. 103.

[26] Ibid., p. 104.

[27] E. A. Burtt, *The Metaphysical Foundations of Modern Physical Science*, 2nd revised edition (London: Routledge and Kegan Paul, 1932), p. 82.

as to what would be the surface of the moon like and whether life could be found there. After some remarks about the severity of lunar conditions, Copernican Salviati noted that any creatures living there would have to be different from terrestrial species, "for this seems to me to fit with the richness of nature and the omnipotence of the Creator and Ruler."[28] Copernican Sagredo assented that those who would make human abilities the measure of what nature can do are extremely rash, for not a single effect in nature is fully understood by anyone.

Certainly Galileo confessed in the *Assayer* that he was almost totally blind when it comes to penetrating the secrets of Nature.[29] An ordered universe is beyond human comprehension. The more his science partook of perfection, the fewer were the conclusions it could demonstrate.[30] Instead of trying to subsume every effect of nature under an all-embracing world system, Galileo contented himself with trying to grasp just a small portion of the magnificent of created phenomena.

Galileo's cautious, intellectual modest rationalism revealed his constant consciousness of a deep appreciation for the richness of nature. Nowhere is this clearer than in his parable of the cicada, about a bird lover

[28] Drake, 1953, p. 101.

[29] Drake, 1957, p. 100.

[30] Drake, 1953, pp. 260 & 189.

who observed the causes of musical sounds. For having captured in his hands a cicada, he failed to diminish its strident noise either by closing its mouth or stopping its wings, yet he could not see it move the scales, which covered its body, or any other part. At last he lifted up the armour of its chest and there he saw thin ligaments beneath, and thinking that the sound might come from their vibration, he decided to break them in order to silence it. But nothing happened until his needle drove too deep, and transfixing the creature he took away its life with its voice, he was still unable to determine whether the song had originated in those ligaments. Now he would never for sure just what the source of the sound had been. From then on when asked how sounds were generated, he would reply that although he knew some of the ways, he was certain many more existed that were unknown and unimaginable. The parable embodied Galileo's conviction that, since God could have created the universe in an infinity of ways.[31] Nature is so bounteous that even our senses and experience were

[31] Galileo drew the moral of the story: "the difficulty of understanding how the cicada's song is formed even when we have it singing to us right in our hand is more than enough to excuse us for not knowing how a comet is formed at such an enormous distance." Drake, 1957, p. 236. The parable takes an inductive phase in which facts are gathered until he is satisfied that the collection is exhaustive. Finally, he is aroused by the startling discovery of yet another way of producing sound, and this leads to the most surprising discovery of all. There is no way of knowing whether nature's ways have been thoroughly investigated. It is only possible to anticipate that what will be known will be expressible in the language of mathematics.

insufficient to teach us the means by which an effect was produced. Precisely because God's thoughts were above ours, nature was not open to human reason at every point.

Galileo did place limits upon our ability to fathom the depths of nature, but this limitation arose from our status as creatures with finite minds rather than from an exercise of God's absoluter freedom. Thus we could not know infinitely many truths, Galileo admitted, for we are not God. We could know discursively by reason some of the truths that God knows instantly by intuition, and here our knowledge was equal to God's. But our limited capacity to comprehend the subtle mathematics of infinity, which God had sometimes used in making the world, meant there were some things about nature we would never fully understand. Indeed one could not prove the precise pattern of the heavens from observations. In a letter to Gallenzone Gallenzoni, Galileo is said to have expressed if it were up to us to arrange the motions of the celestial bodies,

"We should have to rely on proportions of the perfect type, which are the most rational; God, on the other hand, not bothering about symmetries that man can understand, has ordered these motions with the help of proportions that are not only incommensurable and irrational but totally inaccessible to our intelligence."[32]

---

[32] Maurice Clavelin, *The Natural Philosophy of Galileo*, translated by A.J. Pomerans (Cambridge: University of Cambridge Press, 1974), p. 447.

Likewise, Galileo continues, if an architect were to distribute the fixed stars throughout the vault of heaven, he would employ regular geometric figures and familiar ratios that provide the best proportions.[33] But God, by apparently scattering them at random, impresses us as having arranged them without heeding to any rules or any demands of symmetry and elegance. The nature and the finiteness of the world were also beyond human determination. Galileo told Liceti, God's reasons were his own, not man's, and we must not presume to know them. Man could and did, marvel at the size of the universe, but he did not doubt that it had been created for his benefit. The observation of heavenly bodies was respected because it was commonly assumed that human affairs would prosper when undertaken under the right conjunction of stars.

Aristotelian Simplicio takes it for granted that the celestial bodies are ordained to no other use than that of service to the earth. He was amazed by the empty space the Copernicans wished to introduce between Saturn and the stellar sphere. When Aristotelian Simplicio objected that Copernicus put cosmology too vast and too immense, a vast space without anything in between the orbit of Saturn and the fixed stars, was superfluous and vain?

[33] Edward Grant, "Science in the Middle Age" in *The New Catholic Encyclopedia* (San Francisco: McGraw Gill Book Company, 1966), vol. XII. pp. 1200-1209.

For the use and convenience of whom?[34] Salviati, a spokesman of Galileo, replied that "it is brash for our feebleness to attempt to judge the reason for God's actions, and to call everything in the universe vain and superfluous which does serve us."[35] Similarly, Sagredo repeated in the *Dialogue on the World Two Chief Systems*, "to me, a great ineptitude exists on the part of those who would have it that God made the universe more in proportion to the small capacity of their reason than to His immense and His infinite power."[36]

Certainly, God could have decided otherwise. In fact, Galileo wrote that God could have made birds fly with solid gold feathers and fish swim with veins full of quicksilver as proof of His own omnipotence. Instead, their composition followed a teleological necessity: birds have light bones and fish weigh as much as water. Nature's providential order implied the most economical way of acting: "In searching for hidden propositions of how God works, one finds that with respect to what is known, He always complies with the easiest and simplest rules, so that His power could be all

[34] Drake, 1953, p. 367.

[35] Ibid.

[36] Ibid.

the more revealed through His ways."[37] Because God's reasons are inscrutable, it is futile to speculate on what might happen if God, by His absolute power, were to perform an act outside the normal course of nature. If the earth were to stop by God's will, would objects on its surface stop, too? Would the seagull be unable to hover over the fish?

According to Aristotelian Simplicio, if the earth should stop whirling by the will of God, "the birds would do whatever that same will of God desired. All these things would do the opposite from what would be done if, when they were keeping themselves in the air separated from the earth, the terrestrial globe were set unexpectedly in very precipitous motion by God's will."[38] In that case what would happen? If the earth was stopped by God's will, we would see disorders. The seagulls, "that skylarks, though wishing to, would be unable to stay over their nests, nor crows over snails or rocks, so then crows would have to contain their appetite for snails and the young skylarks would perish of hunger and cold, their mother's being no longer able to feed them or to brood them."[39] Galileo's referring to the tides, the ebbing and flowing of the sea can only be caused by motion of the earth

[37] Drake, 1953, p. 370.

[38] Ibid.

[39] Ibid., p. 240.

namely by rotation, Aristotelian Simplico was not convinced and did not therefore consider them true and conclusive. Simplico argued that the ebbs and tide are due to the omnipotent power of God. Therefore the fourth day in the *Dialogue on the Two World Systems*, Simplicio heard from Copernican Galileo and asked

"Whether God in His infinite power and wisdom could have conferred upon the watery element its observed reciprocating motion using other means than moving its containing vessels, that God could have, and that He would have known how to do in many ways which are unthinkable to our minds. This being so, it would be excessive boldness for anyone to limit and restrict the Divine power and wisdom to some particular fancy of his own"[40]

Galileo agreed with this argument of Simplicio and his reply is;

"An admirable and angelic doctrine, and well in accord with anther one, also Divine, which, while it grants us the right to argue about the constitution of the universe (perhaps in order that the working of the human mind shall not be curtailed or made lazy) adds that we cannot discover the work of His hands. Let us, then, exercise these activities permitted to us and ordained by God, that we may recognize and thereby so much the more admire His greatness, however much less fit we may find ourselves to penetrate the profound depths of His infinite wisdom."[41]

We are not sure whether Galileo meant this sincerely because in *Letters on the Sunspots*, he rejected this kind of argument and reasoning.[42]

---

[40] Drake, 1953, p. 464.

[41] Ibid.

[42] Ibid.

One possibility of Galileo's acceptance of Aristotelian Simplicio's argument could be explained only as a conciliatory gesture, so that Galileo could claim falsely that he had obeyed the instruction given to him, not to teach Copernicanism as the true system of the world.

According to Simplicio unless someone could show him a more reasonable cause for the ebb and flow of the sea than Galileo's explanation based on the motion of the earth, he would conclude that it is a supernatural effect. Then Galileo asked Aristotelian Simplicio, "do you not believe that the terrestrial globe could be made moveable supernaturally, by God's absolute power?" Of course, Simplicio answered. And Galileo said since we must introduce a miracle, then, "let us make the earth miraculously move with that motion by which the oceans are naturally moved,"[43] for this would be far simpler and involve fewer miracles than making an immense bulk of water perform all the intricate movements associated with the tides. In case we take this seriously, lest we think that Salviati had adorned himself with his opponent Aristotelian Simplicio's mantle, Galileo added a warning through the mouth of Sagredo: let us not have recourse to miracles unless natural explanations fail. Though Galileo added piously, "to my mind all the

[43] Drake, 1953, p. 464.

work of nature and of God appear miraculous."[44] Galileo's spokesman Salviati feels the same way and with doubtful saying that "the natural cause of the tides is the motion of the earth which does not exclude this operation from being miraculous."[45]

As a matter of fact, Galileo stated that the tides were not miracles but could well be explained in terms of natural forces. Rational analysis could find the cause of natural phenomena. When Aristotelian Simplicio stated that miracle is involved in the rotation of the earth, Galileo rejected. Galileo was of the opinion that human reason could penetrate the mysteries of the universe and we do not have to acclaim them as miracles. Consequently Galileo proclaimed the unlimited power of human reason and gave hope to humanity to strive for a better understanding of the dynamics of nature. Galileo was of the opinion that reason should strengthen faith by eliminating superstitious beliefs. Hence Galileo's science is reconciled with his religion because according to him, observing the splendour of nature itself will lead human mind to the unfathomable beauty of the Creator. Galileo's observations and meditations on God's creation led him to say that the works of nature and of God are miraculous. Galileo often considered on

---

[44] Drake, 1953, p. 464.

[45] Ibid.

what he saw as the stunning manifestations of God's creative wisdom as with birds and their ideal design for flight and fish and their perfect design for swimming in water:

"God could have made birds with bones of massive gold, with veins full of molten silver, with flesh heavier than lead and with tiny wings. He could have made fish heavier than lead, and thus twelve times heavier than water, but He had wished to make the former of bone, flesh, and feathers that are light enough, and the latter as heavier than water, to teach us that He rejoices in simplicity and facility."[46]

Galileo's Ideal of a Deductive Science

The main emphasis of Galileo's theology of creation was on the ability of the human mind to participate in divinity, to read the mathematical language of the perfectly written in the "Book of Nature." This is not to deny that Galileo gave ample room to empirical factors – one must not forget that it was his telescope which first opened the heavens to modern astronomical observation. It is only to assert that his ideal science, the kind of science he advocated from the beginning of his career and brought to full fruition in the *Dialogue Concerning the Two Chief World Systems*, to wit, the science of mechanics, was given at heart much more to deductive demonstration than

[46] Drake, 1953, p. 465.

to inductive investigation. I am not claiming that Galileo's physics divorced reason from reality, mathematics from experience.

Galileo was not a pure abstractionist. Clearly experiment was an essential element in the process of discovery. Yet the role he assigned was a different one. In the context of justification, it took a back seat to necessary mathematical reason. In the incline plan experiment of Galileo, an experimentation of his ideal science, it is Aristotelian Simplicio, the naïve sense empiricist, who calls for an experimental check on the demonstrated conclusions; this experiment is therefore introduced for polemical, not strictly methodological, reason. Copernican Salviati says that true enough experimental proofs are usual and necessary when applying mathematics to the physical world and Galileo himself has not failed to make them. However, Galileo could not have performed some of the experiments he claimed to have performed. This should not be surprising. If, as Galileo repeatedly said, a true science consists only of necessary mathematical demonstrations, it ought to follow that true scientific conclusions require no direct confirmation from experience.

In the *Dialogue on the Two Chief Systems of the World*, when the discussion turns to a stone falling from the mast of a ship, Galileo's spokesman Salviati makes the claim that we know that the stone always falls at the foot of the mast, whether or not the ship is moving. Galileo had in fact done this experiment, at least he said in *Reply to Ingoli*, and there is no reason to doubt it. Simplicio asks whether Salviati, who freely declares the result to be certain, has made the test even once. Salviati replied, "without experiment I am sure that the effect will happen as I tell you, because it must happen that way."[47] Similarly, although Galileo was generally recognized as being one of the founders of the experimental method, many of the experiments referred by him seem only to have been performed mentally or merely stated by him possibly. He often brings in mental experiments or experiments that are only described without being performed. Verification by experiment appears at times to be of secondary importance. As Galileo told Pietro Carcavy, even if it is not the case that experience supports the conclusions, "my demonstrations founded on my supposition lose nothing of their force and conclusiveness. It would matter little whether demonstrated conclusions correspond well to the accidents of nature."[48]

Hardly and surprisingly, Galileo plainly contradicted experience on more than one occasion. For example, it is not true that two pendulums, one with a narrow arc and the other with a wide arc, will swing together for

---

[47] Still Drake, *Galileo at Work: His Scientific Biography* (Chicago: Chicago University Press, 1978), p. 294.

[48] Drake, 1957. p. 320.

hundreds of oscillations, as Galileo claimed in the book of *Discourses*.[49] Nor is it true that if a wooden ball and a lead ball are dropped together, the former at first moves more swiftly than the latter, and then the latter overtakes and passes the former. Yet Galileo explicitly said that he had often tested this. In fairness to Galileo, let me add that he later stated the correct law; nevertheless he did claim experimental verification for this fact. Perhaps the most glaring contradiction of experience was his proof of the earth's motion from the tides. According to Galileo's theory, high and low tides ought to be twelve hours apart.[50] Unfortunately, as every sailor in his country (Italy) knew too well, they are only six hours apart. In his treatise *De motu* (On Motion and on Mechanics), Galileo flatly rejected this fact, calling it a "fallacy which has led writers to imagine many useless fantasies."[51] This shows the a priori nature of Galileo's science.

In the *Dialogue on the Two Chief Systems of the World,* Galileo admitted the six hours interval for the Mediterranean, but attributed it to secondary causes; the primary cause (the earth's double motion) was still

[49] Drake, 1957, p. 226.

[50] The fact that the 'Father of Experimental Science' could make such a mistake after some twenty years of University teaching is perhaps indicative of Galileo's real approach to physical problems.

[51] Shea, p. 177.

credited with producing just one full cycle per day.[52] This is not to deny that observation and experiment had an essential function in Galilean science. Galileo was concerned that the world he was deducing would not be just a world on paper, but the world of our sense experience. There was nothing wrong with thinking of motion and deriving its properties, but he wanted to discover. Galileo wanted to discover the motion which freely falling bodies actually have in nature. He was confident that he had done so, "for the very reason that the essentials successively demonstrated by us correspond to, and are seen to be in agreement with, which physical experiments show forth to the senses."[53] The world could only be mathematical, but which mathematical laws it incorporated was a matter for empirical determination. Galileo held that God endowed us with sense, reason and intellect to give us knowledge. Scriptural texts itself could be interpreted in more than one way.

Galileo on Scriptural Interpretation

The problem confronting Galileo was how to relate the Copernican astronomy with certain passages in the Scripture which seemingly oppose

[52] Shea, p. 118.

[53] Drake, 1957, p. 290.

the heliocentric theory.[54] Galileo was convinced that the Copernican system was true. On the other hand, he had no doubt about the veracity of the Bible. Galileo rightly pointed out that it is possible at first appearance there were contradictions between the Copernican and scriptural texts. But he pointed out that the contradiction arose because of the literal interpretation of such passages in the Scripture. In this context Galileo subscribed to the accommodation theory of interpretation of the Scripture, according to which God in revealing to humans accommodates language.

The accommodation theory of interpretation stated that we must recognize that a real distinction exists between what is said and how it is said. On the other hand, a literal interpretation denies such a distinction and identifies what is said with how it is said. Galileo's position was founded on the basic ideas of his religion. God, the Creator, respects humans created in His own image. God respects also the conditions and the historical situation humans are in when revealing to them. Again, because supremely rational,

---

[54] "Then spoke Joshua to the Lord in the day when the Lord delivered up the Amorites before the children of Israel, and he said in the sight of Israel, Sun stand thou still upon Gibeon; and thou, Moon, in the valley of Ajalon. And the sun stood still, and the moon stayed, until the people had avenged themselves upon their enemies. Is not this written in the book of Jashar? So the sun stood still in the midst of heaven, and hastened not to go down about a whole day." (Joshua. 10: 12-13). The sun's movement is mentioned in other places in the Bible too: In the first chapter of Ecclesiastes. "The sun also arises, and the sun get down, and hasteth to its place where it arises again." (Ecclesiastes 1:55). Isaiah 38:8: "Behold, I will bring again the shadow of the degrees which is gone down in the sun dial of Ahaz, ten degrees backward. So the sun returned ten degrees, by which degrees it was gone down."

God would follow the rational approaches of subordinating means to goal. God would adjust methods of communication in such a way that the message would get across to people most effectively. It can be said that the Bible speaks of the sun's movement because it directs its words to people who think the sun moves, and its aim is not to explain the structure of the heavens. When the miracle God produced for Joshua is described, the point is to explain the greatness of the miracle rather than depict the movement of the sun. The sun seems to be moving, so that we still say that it rises and sets, even though we know that it does not move but rather the earth moves.

Galileo claimed that according to the geocentric theory, one cannot explain the scriptural verses in the book of Joshua by means of an exclusively literal explanation. The sun's movement according to this theory consists of two movements, its annual movement around the earth from east to west, and the daily movement from east to west common to all stars. The movement of the sun is the first movement, while the movement of all stars is the second movement. Thus, if the sun had stopped its motion (west to east), the day would have been shorter, rather than longer.

"Therefore it is absolutely impossible in the system of Ptolemy and Aristotle to stop the motion of the sun and thereby to lengthen the day. Hence either one must say that the motions are not arranged as Ptolemy said, or one must alter the meaning of the words, and say that, when the Scripture says God

stopped the sun, he really wished to say that he stopped the first sphere, the motion of the sun."[55]

Since the literal reading of the scriptural texts does not agree with the geocentric system, we should look for another system, viz., the Copernican heliocentric one. Galileo says that his discovery of the sunspots has proven that the sun rotates on its own axis. Also it is highly probable that the sun is the cause of planetary motion.

"Therefore, if in agreement with the position of Copernicus we attribute the daily rotation primarily to the earth, then who does not see that, in order to stop the whole system without any alteration in the remaining mutual relation of the planets but only to prolong the space and time of the day light, it is sufficient to make the sun stop, exactly as the literal meaning of the sacred text says."[56]

In this way on the basis of the Copernican system it is possible to lengthen the day on earth by stopping the sun, without introducing any chaos among the parts of the world and without altering the words of Scripture. Hence, according to Galileo's interpretation, the sun had only a rotational motion and Joshua's prayer was to stop only this motion. It is clear that Galileo was not content with this line of argument, as is evident from the fact that later on when he took up the interpretation more deeply and

---

[55] Langford, p. 200.

[56] Ibid., p.101.

elaborately in his *Letter to the Grand Duchess Christina*, he never went back to it. The Scripture, to Galileo were divinely inspired and inerrant, though humans can misinterpret their true meaning. The Holy Scripture cannot err and the decrees therein contained are absolutely true and inviolable.

Though Scripture cannot err its expounders and interpreters are liable to err in many ways when they base themselves always on literal meaning of the words. At times the Bible uses figures of speech to simplify concepts which had been inserted into the Bible for the sake of the masses, Galileo insisted, to aid their understanding of matters pertaining to their salvation. In the same way, biblical language had also simplified certain physical effects in Nature, to conform to common experience. Since two truths cannot contradict one another, it is the function of wise expositors of Scripture to seek out the true senses of scriptural texts. These will accord with the physical conclusions of which we are already certain and sure through manifest sense or necessary demonstrations. When one is in possession of knowledge about questions of nature which are not matters of faith, based on indubitable demonstrations or sensory experience, since such knowledge is also a gift from God, one must apply it to the investigation of the true meanings of Scripture in those places which apparently seem to read differently. The meaning of the texts would unquestionably be discovered by theologians, together with the reasons for which the Holy Spirit sometimes wished to veil itself under words with a different meaning. For the Holy Scripture and nature both derive from the Divine Word. Galileo wrote,

"It seems to me that in discussing natural problems we should not begin from the authority of scriptural passages, but from sensory experience and necessary demonstrations. Holy Scripture and nature proceed alike from the Divine Word. Everything that is said in the Bible is not bound by rules as strict as those which govern natural events, and God is no less excellently revealed in these than in the sacred pronouncements of Scripture."[57]

Galileo's interpretation of the scriptural texts makes clear that no truth discovered in nature could contradict the truth of the Holy Scripture. Therefore, one could not contradict the other. He held it dearly that,

"To me the surest and swiftest way to prove that the position of Copernicus is not contrary to Scripture would be to give a host of proofs that it is true and that the contrary cannot be maintained all; thus, since no two truths can contradict one another, this and the Bible must be perfectly harmonious."[58]

Galileo also argued that scientific knowledge could be one of the best aids in interpreting Scripture. The interpretation that Galileo and his

---

[57] Galileo held metaphorically there are two books; book of Nature and book of scripture. The book of nature is written in the language of mathematics, and the book of scripture is scribbled in the language of faith. Galileo and the Bible.*www.galilean-library.org/bible.html*

[58] Langford, p. 87. One must not doubt the possibility that the Divine Goodness at times may choose to inspire a ray of His immense knowledge in low and high intellects, when they are adorned with zeal. Galileo saw himself as the recipient of some such great truths and expressed gratitude to God for being the first to have the revelation: "I render infinite thanks to God, for being so kind as to make me alone the first observer of marvels kept hidden in obscurity for all previous centuries."

contemporaries offered, according to which Scripture may be explained according to scientific knowledge, could have been accepted, as many now accept it today. Theologians in the days of Galileo explained the verses describing the movement of the sun according to the astronomical theories accepted at the time. In order to reinterpret them, it was necessary to explain them in a way that was different from that of theologians. Such an interpretation is possible, as expressed by Cardinal Bellarmine, but is necessary when there are sufficient reasons for it. One such reason would be proof of the earth's motion. If such proof is found, said Bellarmine, it will be necessary to reinterpret these verses according to the scientific discovery. But it is not enough to show that the motion of the earth explains observed phenomena in order to determine that the world indeed works in this way. As many scholars have stated the empirical evidence Galileo could muster fell far short of a demonstrative proof. This never prevents him from asserting that heliocentric theory was true. It is true that Galileo did not fully succeed in integrating science and Scripture on the basis of scientific data, as he had hoped and even claimed; but it is quite clear that this noble task had always been his great ambition.[59]

---

[59] James Brodrick. *Galileo: The Man, His work, His Misfortunes* (London: Geoffrey Campman, 1964), p. 94.

Conclusion

In this chapter, I have tried to demonstrate that Galileo's rationalistic approaches to the laws of natures was the impact of his de-emphasis on Divine freedom. Galileo believed that his mathematical study of the celestial bodies were a matter of decoding the geometrical plan God had employed in the creation. He believed that God had fully thought into the world the very patterns and figures of mathematical forms. Things such as the precise order established in the heavens were forever beyond the reach of human reason. The richness of creation, limited the scope of our inquiry.

Nevertheless it was possible to attain enough certain truths to constitute a demonstrative science of nature. Thus Galileo's natural philosophy was a cautious rationalism. I hope to have shown that God's will had almost no place in Galilean natural philosophy. If God's power was the acknowledged source of nature's bounty, the notion that that power might inhibit our search for causes was laughed out of court. So we find the principal function of Divine omnipotence in Galileo's natural philosophy was implicit, that is to insure that God's thoughts would be realized or embodied in the objects of His making, so that even the celestial bodies in the universe would be subject to the exacting scrutiny of geometry. Since the world was mathematical to the core, our failure completely to know God's work was due more to the defect of a finite understanding than to the exercise of Divine freedom.

As Maurice Clavelin stated "Galileo's rationalism was forced to take stock of its own limitation, that it came to appreciate its true scope and thus armed itself against an oversimplified interpretation of reality."[60] Thus Galileo's theology of creation, like his conception, was essentially rationalistic. The same could be said of Rene Descartes, in emphasizing God's transcendence power, he denied that any limits could be placed on His power to create a boundless universe or eternal truths incomprehensibly different from those that the human mind perceived as necessary.

---

[60] Maurice Clavelin, *Essay on the Origins and Formation of Classical Mechanics* (Cambridge: Cambridge University Press, 1974), p. 447.

CHAPTER TWO

CREATION IN THE NATURAL PHILOSOPHY OF RENÈ DESCARTES

CHAPTER TWO

CREATION IN THE NATURAL PHILOSOPHY OF RENÈ DESCARTES

Introduction

Although natural philosophers of seventeenth century sought validity for their work apart from Divine revelation, divorcing science from religion was something they never intended. In a relation of religion to science in the seventeenth century, we find that a concept of God's Will or Reason played a legitimate role in influencing natural science. In the previous chapter, I have discussed Galileo's emphasis on Divine Reason and His absolute power. We find that Galileo's rationalistic theology of creation was closely linked with his rationalistic science. I have shown that his ideal of scientific knowledge was that of mathematical demonstration, which he believed to be the only way to achieve certainty.

Accordingly Galileo claimed that within the range of mathematical demonstration, human knowledge equals the Divine in objective certainty, for its success in understanding necessity, beyond which there can be no greater sureness. He did place limits upon our ability to plumb the depths of nature, but these limitations arose from our status as creatures with finite minds rather than from an exercise of Divine freedom.

Descartes, like Galileo, was convinced that the human mind was able to comprehend mathematical truths both clearly and distinctly. His natural philosophy, like Galileo's, was deeply informed by rationalistic theology of creation. Descartes insisted that he was discovering the laws of nature that God has made. In the course of his search, Descartes appealed to God as the guarantor of human knowledge. In so doing, he addressed questions about how God created the minds and the world in such a way that certainty in human knowledge is attainable. It is in this context that theological presuppositions played a significant role in his thinking. Descartes' quest for epistemological foundations led him to articulate theological assumptions that bore the imprint of the medieval dialectic about the absolute and ordained power of God.

Descartes believed that after God's initial exercise of absolute power in creating the world, He was bound by the necessity He had freely introduced into the created order. This necessity in the natural world provided Descartes with the warrant he sought for claiming certainty for physics. He grounded his system of knowledge, notably including his natural philosophy, upon the bedrock of God's existence and attributes. It is true that with his radical emphasis on God's will and intellect Descartes denied the distinction on which this chapter will focus, yet his thought exhibits a tension between these two aspects of God's power. At times Descartes takes on the guise of the voluntarist, especially in his declaration that the eternal truths were created by God and could have been otherwise. At other times he appears as the staunch rationalist, constructing a natural philosophy almost entirely from seeds of truth planted in our brains. Thus what were the methodological implications of Descartes' theological assumptions? The answers to these questions lie in the relationship between Descartes' concept of creation and his ideal of a deductive science of nature.

I will first discuss God's attributes which determined for Descartes the nature of the relation between God and the laws of nature, including created minds. Then I shall relate this to his understanding of the relation between the two principal parts of the creation, nature and the human mind. Those attributes which Descartes considered most important were God's infinite perfection, His immense power, and His veracity and immutability as manifested in His infallible decrees.

The Relation between God and the Creation

Descartes was contented to allow God to be God in all of His transcendence. He denied human standards were applicable to God and asserted God's indivisible unity of Will and Reason and unrestricted freedom. In contrast with scholastic tradition, Descartes refused to accept any distinction between God's Will and His Reason – a distinction, which he thought, told nothing of God but reflected purely finite understanding.[1] In reality, he said, God's nature is an indivisible unity of Will and Reason. Therefore God is radically free, His Will is not subject to constraint by His intellect. Descartes wrote in the *Third Meditation*, "it is the nature of the infinite that my nature, which is finite and limited, should not comprehend it."[2] When confronted with the infinite quantities, conventional mathematics was powerless to avoid falling into paradoxes. Any number that we could comprehend could not be infinite, because God alone could be said positively to have no limits in any respect. Descartes reserved for God the term 'infinite.' Other things – numbers, stars, parts of a body, and the

---

[1] Jean Marie Beyssade, "The Idea of God and the Proofs of His Existence", in *The Cambridge Companion to Descartes*, ed. John Cottingham (Cambridge: Cambridge University Press, 1992), pp. 174- 179.

[2] Letter to Mersenne, in *Descartes: Philosophical Letters*, translated by Anthony Kenny, (Oxford: Oxford University Press, 1970), vol. I. p. 166.

extension of the world – were said negatively to be 'indefinite' because they had no discernible limits. And this lack of limits resulted from "the weakness of our understanding rather than from the nature of these things." They could not be construed as limitless in a positive sense. This position, which reflected theological concern, was not without practical benefits for Descartes' natural philosophy. If he denied the motion of the earth, he also denied the infinity of the world more than anyone else.

"We shall find no difficulty in the indefinite extension of the world, if only we would consider that, in saying it is indefinite, we are not denying that perhaps in the very truth of the matter it may be finite, but we are only denying that there are any bounds or extremities which can be comprehended by our intellect."[3]

As Descartes knew, Nicholas of Cusa and others had used this argument for an apparently boundless universe as an expression of God's infinite power. It was intended partially to answer the objection that, in an infinite or at least indefinitely large universe, the place of humanity would be too insignificant and might even render God incapable of special providences. Descartes did not accept this argument. "A finite power," Descartes replied, "might be exhausted by such a world, but the more we esteem the work of God to be great, the more we know the infinity of His

[3] Renè Descartes, *The Principles of Philosophy*, translated by Valentine R. Miller and Reese P. Miller (Boston: Reidel Publications, 1983), p. 91.

power; and the more this infinity is better known to us, the more we are greatly assured it extends to all the particular actions of men."[4] The problem, as Descartes saw it, was not so much with our inadequate conception of God's power as with our exalted conception of our own place in the creation. As Descartes pointed to Burman, men commonly suppose that

"They themselves are the dearest of God's creatures, and that all things are therefore made for their benefit. They think their own dwelling place, the earth, is of supreme importance, that it contains everything that exists, and that for its sake everything was created. But what do we know of what God may have created outside the earth, on the stars and so on?"[5]

Descartes did not reject final causes, but he rejected the claim that we can know the final causes of natural things, because it is impossible for us to know God's purposes: "we ought not be so arrogant as to think that we are participant in his plans."[6] Despite this fragment evidence that Descartes held teleological views, he explicitly stated that final causes had no roles in physics, and they played no role in his mechanical explanations of various phenomena in the way that they had in traditional Aristotelian natural philosophy. Even if we could know the purpose of a thing, arguing from

---

[4] Anthony Kenny, "The Cartesian Circle and the Eternal Truths," in *Journal of Philosophy* 67(1970): 685-700.

[5] *Renè Descartes' Philosophical Letters*, translated by Anthony Kenny, (Oxford: Oxford University Press, 1970), vol. I. p. 166.

[6] Ibid.

ends, which was Aristotelian fault, could never lead to the knowledge of the thing itself.[7] Nowhere is Descartes' confession of God's absolute power more apparent than in his doctrine of the eternal truths for example, "the whole is greater than its part," "two plus two equals four."[8] Descartes' views on the eternal truths are found in his replies to the fifth and sixth sets of objection in the *Conversation with Burman*. In the following section I will discuss Descartes' general position of eternal truth which is opposed to the prevailing conception in which both God and man were bound by unchangeable laws in nature.

God's Absolute Power over the Eternal Truths

It is Descartes' metaphysical ideas about God that formed the foundations of his natural philosophy. In *Principles of Philosophy*, Descartes defined God as an infinite, eternal, immutable, omnipotent God by which all existing things have been created. With regards to God's absolute power,

---

[7] Kenny, vol. II. p. 174. Gasendi's objection to Descartes' amputation of final causes from physics is found in Objections and Replies V: *Philosophical Works of Descartes:* Descartes' replied is on page 222, in which he stated that "we cannot pretend that certain of God's purposes rather than others are openly displayed; all seems to be equally hidden in the abyss of His inscrutable wisdom."

[8] Kenny, vol. I. p. 22.

Descartes held that

"The mathematical truths which we can call eternal have been laid down by God and depend on Him no less than the rest of His creatures. Indeed to say that these truths are independent of God is to talk of Him as if God were Jupiter or Saturn and to subject Him to the fates. In general we can assert that God can do anything that we can comprehend but not that He cannot do what we cannot comprehend. It would be rash to think that our imagination reaches as far as His power."[9]

Descartes could not accept any views which subordinated God's Will to His reason or failed to distinguish between our finite minds and God's infinite mind. He refused to allow anything could be independent of God. Unconstrained by anything else in the universe, he presented "the eternal truths did not exist in any sense apart from God because He had willed them to be so, for the existence of God is first and most eternal of all possible truths and the one from which alone all others derive."[10] As the efficient cause of all things, as the Creator and the source of both the essence and the existence of every creature, God had created the eternal truths freely. God was free in creating the world to do anything, whether or not its description is logically coherent. Descartes also evidently thinks that God, while creating the essence 'circularity,' could have made it different from what we conceive it to be. In that case there would be eternal truths about circles, but

[9] Letter to Mersenne, 6 May 1630, in *Renè Descartes: Philosophical Letters*, translated by Anthony Kenny, (Oxford: Clarendon Press, 1970), vol. I. p. 11.

[10] http://www.drury.edu/ess/philsci/Descartes.html

they would differ from – and perhaps be the negations of – the propositions that are necessarily true of circularity as we now understand it. And just as God was free not to create the world, (which shows that Descartes' God has no reason behind his creative acts) so also He was no less free to make it untrue that the line drawn from the center of a circle to its circumference are equal.[11] God's creative acts had been radically free, undetermined by any considerations whatsoever, that is there were no external constraints which in any way restricted His creative act. On the other hand, once having exercised God's Will with absolute freedom, God could not alter the eternal truths. It was how Descartes describes in his reply to the sixth set of objections to the *Meditations*,

"God did not will to create the world in time because he saw that it would be thus than if he had created it from all eternity; nor did he will that the three angles of a triangle should be equal to two right angles because he recognized that it could be otherwise and so on. On the contrary, it is because he willed to create the world in time that it is better this way than if he created it from eternity; and it is because he willed that the three angles of a triangle should necessarily equal two right angles that this is true and cannot be otherwise; and so on in other cases."[12]

As shown by the citation, identifying the divine understanding and the Divine Will leads Descartes to the view that God's freedom consists in

---

[11] Kenny, vol. I. p. 10.

[12] Kenny, vol. II. p. 248.

absolute indifference. Since there are no truths prior to God's creation of them, His creative Will cannot be determined or even moved by any considerations of rationality whatever. "It is admissible," Descartes declared, "that God's Will has not been indifferent from all eternity to everything that has been or ever will be done." The Divine Will is, in other words, entirely arbitrary. There are no priori conditions of right or reason to which it must conform; indeed, there are none to which it might choose to conform.

In his *"Reply to Objections VI"* Descartes maintained that if anyone attends to the immeasurable immensity of God he will find that nothing at all can exist which does not depend on Him. Nothing precedes creation, nothing determines the free act, not even anything within God himself. Only then can God be said to be omnipotent in the strongest sense. Descartes has often been taken to be, on the basis of those assertions, an extreme voluntarist. If, however, by voluntarism one means the proposition that God's Will precedes His understanding, Descartes is, as Menn and Marion both argue, no voluntarist. He insists instead on the unity of the Divine Will and Intellect. There is in God neither knowing without willing nor willing without knowing. The Divine Command, "Let there be light", is at once the act by which light came to be and also the act by which God, in creating its essence, knew it, and knew also that it was good, as Descartes says, citing Genesis.

Descartes maintains that to one who pays attention to God's immensity, it is clear that nothing at all can exist which does not depend on Him. This is true not only of everything that subsists, but of all order, of every law, and of every reason of truth and goodness; for otherwise God, as has been said just before, would not have been wholly indifferent to the creation of what he has created. For if any reason for what is good had preceded his preordination, it would have determined Him towards that which it was best to bring about. But on the contrary because He determined Himself towards those things which ought to be accomplished, for that reason, as it stands in Genesis, they are very good; that is to say, the reason for their goodness is the fact that He wished to create them so. Nor is it worth asking in what class of cause fall that goodness or those other truths, mathematical as well as metaphysical, which depend on God; for since those who enumerated the classes of cause did not pay sufficient attention to causality of this type, it would have been by no means strange if they had given it no name. Nevertheless they did give it a name; for it can be styled efficient causality in the same sense as the king is the efficient cause of the laws, although a law is not a thing which exists physically, but is merely as they say [in the Schools] a moral entity. Again it is useless to inquire how God could from all eternity bring it about that it should be untrue that twice four is eight, etc, for Descartes admit that that cannot be understood by us.

Yet, on the other hand, since we understand that nothing in any category of causation can exist which does not depend upon God and that it would have been easy for Him so to appoint that we human beings should not understand how these very things could be otherwise than they are, it would be irrational to doubt concerning that which we correctly understand, because of that which we do not understand and perceive no need to understand. Hence we should not think that eternal truths depend on the human understanding or on other existing things; they must depend on God alone, who, as the supreme legislator, ordained them from all eternity.[13] The eternal truths depend (for their truth, etc.) on His deity, who could have made them untrue—that is to say, presumably, that this deity could have made contradictions of truth.

Descartes held the belief that God is the Ruler of creation whose sovereignty imposed laws of His own choice, the products of His free will and not of a rational necessity external to Himself. In contrast to David Derodon who held that God chooses the best among the possibilities that his

[13] Kenny, vol. II. pp. 250 - 251.

reason presents to his will, Descartes' God had had complete freedom of indifference, to the extent that no ordinary logic had limited his creative acts. For Descartes, God's omnipotence required him to be able to perform even what we understand to be logically impossible. The eternal realities were no less contingent than any other propositions which God could have freely willed to create. This means that God was free in creating the world to do anything, whether or not its description is logically coherent. God could have made it untrue that twice four is eight or that the angles of a triangle equal a straight line. If He had done so, however, the minds He in fact gave us would be incapable of comprehending it.

The act of creation, a product of God's absolute power, established the order of nature, because of the immutability of His will, God maintains and conserves in the manner in which He first created it. The ensuring necessity of the law is a necessity relative to this natural order and to our understanding of it. Therefore it can be understood in terms of God's ordained power.

Descartes pointed out that God is free and that His Will is immutable. Any cognitive dissonance that we experience in the face of these two propositions, God is free and that His Will is immutable, is not evidence that one of them is false but evidence that we do not fully understand how the power of an immutable being amounts to omnipotence. For a better understanding of this, we may adhere to Descartes' *Fourth Meditation* rule for judging and not make affirmations about it. A common reading of Descartes has him holding that God's omnipotence guarantees that God could have done other than what He has in fact done. Among the passages that are most suggestive of this reading are the ones in which Descartes puts forward his famous doctrine of the creation of the eternal truths: "God is free to make it untrue that twice four is eight or that one and two make three, though if He had done so, the minds He in fact gave us would incapable of comprehending it, for God has created our minds so as to be able conceive as possible, things which God has wished to be in fact possible, but not those things which God could have made possible."[14] And even if God has willed that some truths should be necessary, this does not mean that He willed them necessarily; for it is one thing to will that they are necessary and quite another to will them necessarily, or to be necessitated to will them."[15] Descartes would not dare to say that God cannot make a mountain without a

[14] Harry Frankfurt, "Descartes on the Creation of the Eternal Truth," in *The Philosophical Review* 86(1977): 36.

[15] Kenny, vol. II. p. 151.

valley, or to bring it about that one plus two are not three.[16] It would be rash indeed to think that our imagination reaches as far as His power.

But there was still one thing which even God could not do. He could not act against His own perfect nature, for then He would not be God. Although God could, by His absolute power, have made it untrue that two plus two is four, for that would be an imperfection. Hence there were two kinds of eternal truths in Descartes' philosophy. The uncreated eternal truths, which could not be otherwise, flowed necessarily from God's essence, and the created eternal truths, free products of the Divine will, appear to the human mind to be necessary but could have been otherwise if God had so willed.[17] The uncreated eternal truths were not subject to change – they were in fact eternal.[18] But what of the created truths? If they were dependent on God's unfettered Will and not upon reason, how could they be eternally valid, and how could they possibly be discovered by the human

---

[16] David Cunning, "Descartes on the Immutability of the Divine Will," in *Religious Studies* 39 (2003): 82.

[17] Ibid. 92. Daving Cunning further divides the uncreated eternal truths into a single most eternal truth – that God exists – and several more eternal truths of the Divine being and nature.

[18] B. Funkenstein, *Theology and Scientific Imagination* (Princeton: Princeton University Press. 1985), p.150. Amos Funkenstein has argued that Descartes did not exempt God from the principle of contradiction, but rather he allowed God to determine what for us would constitute a contradiction. The eternal truths, as free product of the Divine will, appeared to the human mind to be necessary but could have been otherwise if God had so willed.

mind?. The answer to these questions would be seen in Descartes' understanding of God's attributes, especially His perfection about which I have discussed below.

Perfection and Immutability

God not only created the eternal truths, He also created our minds in such a way that we posses an innate capacity to understand them. Descartes introduced an element of necessity into the world, the connection between the eternal truths and our minds. The idea of God is the foundation of Descartes' science: he held that God created the eternal truths (i.e., the mathematical truths) and the laws of nature and stated his view, "there is no single one (of the eternal truths) that we cannot understand if our mind turns to consider it. They are all inborn in our minds, just as a king would imprint his laws on the hearts of all his subjects if he had enough power to do so."[19] If the eternal truths are somehow inborn in our minds, how can we be assured that God will not change them, and that we will not be deceived in believing them to be true? Descartes held that God's Will is immutable. God's perfection involves not only His being is immutable in Himself, but

[19] *Renè Descartes: Philosophical Letters*, translated by Anthony Kenny (Oxford: Oxford University Press, 1970), p. 11.

also God is operating in a manner that is always constant and immutable. With regard to this Descartes express to defend his doctrine against the charge that created truths will not be eternal. He expressed to Mersenne,

"It will be said that if God had established eternal truths He could change them as a king changes his laws. To this the answer is; yes He can, if His will can change. But I understand them to be eternal and unchangeable. I make the same judgment about God. But His will is free. Yes, but His power is incomprehensible. And generally we can be well assured that God can do all that we can understand, but not that He cannot do what we cannot understand."[20]

The principle is restated much later in letters to Henry More. There is but one condition on God's Will. It will be immutable. We must suppose, given the absolute indifference with which God acts, that immutability is not a principle by which God's acts are guided. It must instead follow from the Divine nature itself. The eternal validity of the created truths obviously depends upon the immutability of God's Will, for if He were able to change His Will, God would be able to change the eternal truths or the laws of nature. But God was for Descartes an inseparable unity of Will and Reason. In contrast with scholastic tradition, but in keeping with his emphasis on Divine transcendence, Descartes refused to accept any distinction between God's Will and His Reason – a distinction, Descartes thought, which told nothing of God but reflected purely human limitation. In reality, Descartes

[20] Kenny, vol. II. p. 11.

said, "God's nature was an indivisible unity of will and reason."[21] Therefore a change in God's Will would entail a change in His understanding. However a change in His understanding would be an imperfection, since at some time his understanding would have been mistaken or incomplete; therefore God's Will could not change.[22] "Concerning the decrees of God which have already been enacted," as Descartes told Burman, "it is clear that God is unalterable with regard to these, and from the metaphysical point of view, it is impossible to conceive the matter otherwise."[23] Thus, although Descartes did not think that "the essence of things, and those mathematical truths which may be known about them, are independent of God,"[24] he nevertheless affirmed "that because God so wished it and brought it to pass, they are immutable and eternal."[25] Writing to Princess Elizabeth, Descartes' reiterated Divine immutability precludes any change in God's Will:

"When your highness speaks of the particular providence of God as being the foundation of theology, I do not think that you have in mind some change in God's decrees occasioned by actions that depend on our free will. No

---

[21] Miller, p.12

[22] Blom, p.163.

[23] Osler, p. 32. Descartes discussed the efficacy of prayer in light of God's immutable decrees, concluding that God is indeed unalterable, and that He has decreed from eternity either to grant us a particular request or not to grant it.

[24] Kenny, vol. I. p. 226.

[25] Kenny, vol. II. p. 226.

such change is theologically tenable, and when we are told to pray to God, that is so that we should inform him of our needs, or that we should try to get him to change anything in the order established from all eternity by his providence – either of these aims would be blameworthy – but simply to obtain whatever he has, from all eternity, willed to be obtained by our prayers."[26]

In other words, God's design for the world, maintained by His ordained power, is not subject to further change, even by His absolute power. This position separates Descartes from the voluntarist, who insisted that God is absolutely free to change any of His decrees, and the laws of nature are contingent on His Will. Descartes' argument reflected the traditional discourse about the absolute and ordained power of God. By His absolute power, God freely created the eternal truths, just as He freely created the other creatures. In this act of creation, God's power and freedom were absolute, unconstrained by anything else in the universe.

Nothing in the universe exists independent of God, even the laws of mathematics. The eternal truths are true because God knows them. It is not the case that God knows them because they are true, for in that case the absolute truth would exist independent of His creative act.[27] For Descartes,

[26] Kenny, vol. II. p. 273.

[27] Descartes' view is in sharp contrast with the position of scholastic intellectualists such as that of Francisco Suárez, that the eternal truths are not true because they are known by God, rather they are known because they are true, otherwise no reason could be given why God necessarily knows that they are true, for if their truth proceeded from God

nothing can necessitate, or even incline without necessitating, God to perform any given creative act.

As for the eternal truth, Descartes said they are all true or possible only because God knows them as true or possible. They are not known as true by God in any way which would imply that they are true independently of Him. If men understood the sense or meaning of their words they could never say without blasphemy that the truth of anything is prior to the knowledge which God has of it. In God, willing and knowing are a single thing in such a way that by the very act of willing something, He knows it, and it is for this reason that such a thing is true. So we must not say that if God did not exist nonetheless these truths would be true. For the existence of God is foremost and the one from which all others derived.

It is notably that the existence of God is an uncreated eternal truth, but obviously not one that in any way limits God's freedom. Accordingly we find that Descartes thought that the laws of nature, which are the first principles of his natural philosophy, possess precisely the epistemological status, a status that is closely related to his understanding of the eternal truths. Descartes' laws of nature stated that God is the first cause of motion. God by His omnipotence created matter with motion and now conserves in

---

himself, that would happen by means of God's will, so it would not proceed necessarily but voluntarily.

the universe by His ordained power as much motion and rest as He placed in it while creating it.[28] Here it reflected the discourse about the two powers of God. By His absolute power, God created matter and motion; by His ordained power, God conserves them. That is, God relies on the natures and second causes He created to bring about particular effects. Descartes' justification for this statement rests on one of the Divine attributes, in this case immutability. He stressed God's immutable nature as one of His perfections. It was Divine perfection to be immutable and constant in the way God acts. Just because God conserves the laws, it does not follow that they must be conservation laws.

Nevertheless, the laws of nature, as Descartes stated them in *The Principles of Philosophy*, have the same epistemological status as the eternal truths. Part of the initial creation, they possess the same kind of necessity as the eternal truths, a necessity following from Divine immutability. Descartes' laws of nature were far from the view of voluntarist's, according to which the laws of nature are contingent on Divine Will and God can alter them at will. We also know that it is a perfection in God, not only that He is immutable in His nature, but also that it is the question of a mode which He never changes: such that besides the changes which we see in the world, and

[28] Osler, p. 137.

those which we believe because God has revealed them and which we know happen or have happened in nature, without any change on the part of the Creator, we ought not to suppose that there are any others in His work, for fear of attributing inconstancy to Him. From this it follows that it is consistent with reason for us to think that since God moved the different parts of matter in several different ways when He created them, and since God always maintains them in the same way and with the same laws which He made them obey at His creation, God ceaselessly maintains in it an equal quantity of motion.[29]

Descartes' understanding of Divine immutability was a curious one indeed, embracing not only God's nature but also His actions. The law of motion, as Descartes held in *Le Monde*, follows from the fact that "God is immutable and that, acting always in the same way, God always produces the same effect."[30] To hold that God's nature and Will did not change was orthodox, but to hold in addition that God always acts in the same way was not the usual interpretation. Even John Calvin, who staunchly defended the constancy of God's will, admitted that God's action could change.[31]

---

[29] Osler, p. 58.

[30] Ibid., p. 36.

[31] Speaking of the constancy of God's will, Calvin said that "we ought not to understand anything else under the word "repentance' than change of action, because men wont by

For Descartes, however, God's immutability meant the constancy of God's action in the world as manifested in the conservation of quantity of motion, whereby God maintained every motion precisely as it was at that moment, and not as it had been an instant before.[32] God was, therefore, the active efficient cause of motion just as He was "the cause of creating things, not only in respect of their coming into being, but also in respect to their continued existence."[33] This is consistent with Descartes' statement that God's ordained power did not differ from His absolute power, a statement Descartes made in his reply to the *Sixth Objection in the Meditation.* For Descartes, then, the laws of nature were not simply decrees, they were enactments whereby God immutably and universally sustained what He had fully determined.

---

changing their action to testify that they are displeased with themselves. Therefore, since every change among men is correction of what displeases them, but that correction arises out of repentance, then by the word 'repentance' is meant the fact that God changes with respect to his actions. Meanwhile neither God's plan nor his will is reversed, nor his volition altered; but what he had from eternity foreseen, approved, and decreed, he pursues it uninterrupted in men's eyes." John Calvin, *Institutes of the Christian Religion*, (London: SCM Press, 1960), vol. 1. p. 227. Descartes' view of prayer was not very different from this, but Calvin seems to have been unperturbed by the notion of God acting in different ways at different times – always, of course, in harmony with his immutable decrees.

[32] Miller, pp. 58-61. Descartes was following the Christian- Aristotelian practice of connecting a phenomenon directly to one of God's attributes.

[33] Ibid., p. 219.

Descartes showed that the laws of nature were and without basing his argument on any principle other than the infinite perfection of God, he tried to demonstrate all those laws about which we could have any doubt, and to show that they are such that, even if God created many worlds, there could not be any in which they failed to be observed. Our knowledge of God's attributes enables us to have a priori knowledge of the laws of nature. These laws, however, are general, so general that they would apply to any world that God might have created. This conclusion flow from the Divine power. Any of the worlds that God might create would be governed by the same laws of nature because the nature and existence of God are uncreated eternal truths and therefore universally applicable.[34]

In spite of his conception of God's ordained power, and God's action in nature, Descartes limited God's power over the creation.[35] He held that by His absolute power, God created matter and set the parts of matter in motion in the beginning, and by His ordained power, God preserves the same quantity of motion in the universe. As Descartes described them in *The Principles of Philosophy*, the laws of nature have the same epistemological status as the eternal truths. Part of the initial creation, they posses the same

---

[34] J. D. Collins, *Renè Descartes' Natural Philosophy of Nature* (Oxford: Basil Blackwell, 1971). pp. 27 & 48.

[35] Ibid., p. 77.

kind of necessity as the eternal truths, a necessity which flows from Divine immutability. Descartes' laws of nature were far from Robert Boyle's that God is free to alter the laws of nature at Will. Descartes also mitigated God's sovereignty believing that while the regular laws of nature were the direct result of Divine superintendence of motion, the actual, irregular paths of particulars were produced by the diverse nature of matter, for which God was apparently not responsible. At one point Descartes was willing to entertain the thought that God might have created the world in a state of chaos from which He brought order by His laws, but later he abandoned this as unbecoming of the character of God.[36]

God and Human Knowledge: Certainty and Innate Ideas

In this section, I call attention to what did Descartes have to say about the status of the eternal truth? Descartes asserted that eternal truths like everything else in the world have been freely created by God. The laws of nature can be understood as the products of God's absolute power. Descartes' understanding of eternal truths and his knowledge of them is contained in his much-quoted letter to Mersenne.

---

[36] Olscamp, p. 35.

"Do not hesitate to assert and proclaim everywhere that it is God who has laid down laws in nature just as a king lays down laws in his kingdom. There is no law that we cannot understand if our mind turns to consider it. They are all inborn in our minds just as a king would imprint his laws on the hearts of all his subjects if he had enough power to do so."[37]

To think of the eternal truth as existing independently of God would be a blasphemous affront to Divine omnipotence. God is not limited by anything in the world. In this act of creation, God exercised His absolute power. He was free to create or not to create the eternal truths. If it is one thing to assert that God made certain propositions true for all eternity, it is another to assert that our mind is capable of discovering them and of recognizing them as truths. In the *Third Meditation*, Descartes admitted that

"It would be easy for God to deceive us by giving us minds that mistake false propositions for the truth. But when I took anything very simple and easy in the sphere of arithmetic or geometry into consideration, e.g. two and three together made five, and other things of the sort, were not these present to my mind so clearly as to enable me to affirm that they were true? Certainly if I judged that since such matters could be doubted, this would not have been so for any other reason than that it came into my mind that perhaps a God might have endowed me with such a nature that I may have been deceived even concerning things which seemed to me most manifest. But every time that this preconceived opinion of the sovereign power of a God presents itself to my thought, I am constrained to confess that it is easy to Him, if God wishes it, to cause me to err, even in matters in which I believe myself to have the best evidence."[38]

---

[37] Kenny, vol. I. p.11.

[38] Miller, p. 158. Descartes said "it seems to me that I now have before me a road which will lead us from the contemplation of the true God, in whom the treasures of science and wisdom are contained, to the knowledge of the other objects of the universe."

The God who created us could do all things, as Descartes acknowledged in *Principles of Philosophy* and "we do not know whether He choses to make us in such a way that we are always mistaken, even about those things which appear to us to be the best known of all."[39] But the God who created us was also perfect, which meant, as Descartes argued in the *Fourth Meditation*, that it is impossible that He should ever deceive us. For in fraud and deception some imperfection is to be found. And although it may appear that the power of deception is a mark of subtlety or power, yet the desire to deceive without doubt testifies to malice or feebleness, and accordingly cannot be found in God.[40] This proposition, "God cannot lie, was the foundation of faith and belief," Descartes told Mersenne.[41] Those theologians who denied it, in opposition to Augustine and Aquinas, would have to abandon all certainty - something which Descartes was hardly about to allow. Therefore he appealed to the veracity of God, from which it followed that everything we perceive is clearly true, beyond any possibility of doubt, or else God would be a deceiver. Thus our conceptions of the eternal truths of mathematics and other propositions perceived clearly and

[39] Miller, p. 4.

[40] Kenny, Vol. II. p. 172.

[41] Ibid., p. 99.

distinctly were in fact true.[42] As the Ruler of creation, Descartes expressed to Mersenne, God had implanted in the human mind certain 'innate' ideas, 'such as the idea of God, mind or soul, body, triangle, etc., and in general all those which represent true immutable and eternal essences," that is, the eternal truths.[43]

Descartes' belief in God's absolute sovereignty led him to ask whether there could be any necessary truths if God is not bound by human standards. But having denied that God was subject to rational constraint whatsoever, Descartes argued that He could not act against His own nature by changing His mind, so that whatever God had freely chosen to make true would remain true for all eternity. God is free not to create the eternal truths in the sense that nothing determines Him to create the eternal truths that He in fact creates. Still God cannot change His will, and nothing other than God can change His Will, and so in a sense it is possible for God to have not created the eternal truths that are with us. We might doubt the truth of any proposition except the proposition that the ability to doubt implied the

---

[42] Oscamp, p. 32.

[43] Ibid., p. 33. In the *Third Meditation*, Descartes stated, "The idea of God was the mark of the workman imprinted on His work, the very image (imago dei) of God." In the early *Regulae*, Descartes had spoken of "certain primary germs of truth implanted by nature" rather than implanted directly by God." Kenny, vol. I. p. 12. Descartes' expression in the *Third Meditation* is more explicitly theistic.

existence of the doubter; the clarity and distinctness of this undubitable truth became the cornerstone for the edifice of certain knowledge. Thus the genius who haunted the sleep of reason was nothing other than God shorn of His veracity, the creator of arbitrary and continually changing essences, and doubt was transformed into the means for arriving at eternal truths. In the absence of prejudices – to wit, all men would clearly perceive the same set of eternal truths, the very essences ordained by God, Descartes boldly expressed in *Principles of Philosophy* 1.50.[44]

What is more, if we were unable to conceive of something without finding a contradiction in our conception, we could then conclude that it did not exist at all,[45] which is just what Descartes did with regard to atoms and the void. Although Descartes maintained that the properties of objects were a function of the way their minute parts were put together, he did not think that all matter was made up in the end of impenetrable and irreducible atoms.[46] Since for Descartes, the reality of the world is what can be described numerically, it follows that just as there is no smallest possible

---

[44] Miller, p. 22.

[45] For there is no doubt that God possesses the power to produce everything that we are capable of perceiving with distinctiveness, and we have never deemed that anything was impossible for Him, unless we found a contradiction in attempting to conceive it clearly.

[46] Kenny, vol. II, p. 185.

number, so there can be no smallest possible particle, or atom. Matter, therefore, must be infinitely divisible. For the same reason, Descartes denied the possibility of a vacuum. If the true description of the world is its mathematical description, and matter just is its dimensions (extension), then a space between objects, since it possesses size, duration and motion, is every bit as real a physical thing as are the objects on either side of it.

Descartes held that there is therefore no such thing as genuinely empty space: just as a room which the common person would say was empty is known by the philosopher to be full of air. Descartes could not conceive of the idea of body was contained in the idea of space no less than the idea of a mountain was contained in the idea of a valley. To imagine that God removes all the air in a room without putting any other body in its place, as Descartes wrote to Mersene, "you will have to suppose that the walls of the room will touch each other; otherwise you will be thinking a self contradictory thought."[47] Hence a vacuum was impossible. Because matter and extension were inseparable, an atom was necessarily an extended body which was clearly and distinctly divisible, and anything had in fact to be divisible, at least by God if not by human agents. So atoms could not exist either. The same issue was expressed in Descartes' letter to Arnauld and

[47] Miller, p. 22.

More in 1649. In both the letters, Descartes tempered his earlier position (in *the Principles*) conceding that he could not place limits on God's absolute power to perform a contradiction. But the thrust of each of the passages was to affirm in different ways that Descartes could not comprehend such an act, he was concerned, it could not be a liked possibility, as Descartes said in his reply to the authors of the *Sixth Objections*,

"It is useless to inquire how God could from all eternity bring it about that it should be untrue that twice four is eight;" it would be irrational to doubt concerning that which we correctly understand, because of that which we do not understand and perceive no need to understand."[48]

Doubt gave way to practical certainty. In the last resort, as Hooykaas has noted, "human reason became the measuring rod for the truth of existence!"[49]

The Relationship Between Created Minds and Created Objects

Descartes recognized that the possibility of certain knowledge depended on the knowledge of God. Once God was known in all of His

---

[48] Miller, p. 251.

[49] Reijer Hooykaas, *Religion and the Rise of Modern Science* (Grand Rapids: Eerdmans, 1972), p. 42. Hooykass analysis ring true. "There cannot be a void, not because God could not have made it, but because He does not will it to be, and he knows this because our reason cannot conceive how a void could possibly exist."

veracity and constancy, he thought it was possible to achieve full and certain knowledge of countless matters, both concerning God himself and other intellectual matters, also concerning of those matters which pertain to corporeal nature which is the subject matter of pure mathematics. Therefore Descartes sought to derive his philosophy from the knowledge of God, in so far as it was possible. Among various interpretations, one of them is that Descartes' method in natural philosophy was determined by passages which one takes as normative. I agree with the bulk of Cartesian thought in taking the Sixth part (rather than the second part) of the *Discourse on Method* as his most definitive statement. Descartes states:

"First, I tried to discover the general principles, or first causes, of all that is or can be in the world, without for this purpose considering anything but God alone, its Creator, and without deriving these principles from anything but certain seeds of truth which are naturally in our souls."[50]

In spite of appearances, Descartes did not see himself as an ivory tower philosopher who built a world on paper according to his personal whims. The existing world is what he wanted to explain, and this could not be done with imaginary principles established through the impulse of several armchair thinkers. It was nevertheless true that, as G.A. J Rogers has stated,

[50] Olscamp, p. 52.

a large part of Cartesian physics could be done in an armchair.[51] With the perfection of God as his starting point, Descartes believed he could deduce the laws of motion and the eternal truths of mathematics. He tried to "demonstrate all those laws about which we might have any doubt, and to show that they are such that even if God had created many worlds, there would have been none of them where these laws failed to be observed."[52]

Descartes argued,

"Knowledge of those laws are so natural to our souls that we cannot but judge them infallible when we conceive them distinctly, nor doubt that, if God had created many worlds, the laws would be as true in all of them as in this one. Thus, those who can examine sufficiently the consequences of these truths and of our rules will be able to know effects by their causes and (to explain myself in the language of the schools) will be able to have demonstrations a priori of everything that can be produced in that new world."[53]

For Descartes, then, it was not enough merely to know laws that described or explained selected phenomena. The laws of physics had to be necessary truths, valid and capable of yielding certain knowledge through a priori demonstration. If God did indeed create many worlds, each with its own sun, there was only one kind of world, one which our mind could

[51] Olscamp, p. 29.

[52] Ibid., p. 35.

[53] Kenny, vol. II. p. 75.

penetrate because God had established certain truths both in the world and in our minds. Only the certainty of mathematics was acceptable to Descartes. Unless it could be deduced from indubitable common notions with mathematical demonstration, a proposition could not be accepted as true. Even this was not enough. If Descartes could only say how things could be, without showing that they could not be otherwise, Descartes preferred to think he knew nothing.[54]

The Deductive Ideal and God's Creative Power

This is not to say that Descartes' physics was mathematical – its sparse use of mathematics was perhaps its flaws. But rather that mathematics was for him the paradigm of science, the model of certain knowledge. Descartes admired mathematics not so much for its content as for its method of moving from one proposition to another, by which the certainty of the antecedent flowed undiminished down to the consequent. Perceived clearly and distinctly by the light of reason alone, the innate ideas functioned as

[54] Miller, p. 76. As I have discussed in the previous chapter, similar sentiments were expressed by Galileo, who also took mathematics to be the exemplar of scientific knowledge.

seeds of truth from which the tree of knowledge grew.[55] Now for Descartes, deduction was not limited to syllogistic reasoning, but included any sequence of propositions in which could be perceived clear and distinct relation between the premises and the conclusion. At least in part, deduction was process whereby intuition moved to extend itself to embrace previously uncertain notions. It is the natural light of reason, not the form of the argument, which established the validity of a proposition.[56]

Descartes conceived his physics and science more generally as resting on the metaphysical foundation. For him, the content of relevant metaphysics concerns most especially the knowledge of God and of one's self. Thus having established the laws of nature by reason rather than from the senses, so that they were true beyond question, Descartes went on to consider whether they were adequate to explain natural phenomena.[57] He believed that they were, at least for explaining the general structure of the world. Proceeding to reconstruct the world, Descartes examined what were

---

[55] Miller, p. 249. "All philosophy is like a tree, of which the roots are metaphysics, the trunk is physics, and the branches coming form this trunk are all the other sciences and I tell you, between us, that these six Meditations contain all the foundation of my physics."

[56] A. B. Gibson, *The Philosophy of Descartes* (New York: Barnes Books, 1980), p. 155.

[57] Miller, p. 80.

the first and most ordinary effects that we could infer from those causes. He stated,

"It seems to me that I thereby discovered the skies, the stars, an earth, and even, on the earth, water, air, fire, minerals, and certain other such things, which are the commonest and simplest of all, and thus the easiest to understand."

First and most effects mentioned in this statement were the basic parts of the heavens and the earth, the subject of *Le Monde*, though later, in the *Principles of Philosophy*, Descartes seems to have limited them to celestial phenomena alone. Whatever they were, Descartes claimed to have discovered them, by which he could only have meant that he had derived them from the first causes of everything, so that their causes had been found. Descartes believed that he had found such causes for the general effect cannot be questioned. Assuredly, he said,

"If the principles I use are very obvious, if I deduce nothing from them except by means of a mathematical sequence, and if what I deduce is in exact agreement with all natural phenomena; it seems (to me) that it would be an injustice to God to believe that the causes of the effects which are in nature and which we have thus discovered are false. For we would then be accusing Him of having made us so imperfect as to be liable to make mistakes, even when correctly using our reason (which God has given us)."[58]

For Descartes, then, science was rooted in metaphysics, a true philosophy, and achieved certain knowledge of nature by holding to what I

[58] Miller, p. 104.

will call the deductive ideal: from indubitable first principles derived from the Divine perfection and immutability, one could deduce the world and all that is therein. But God was more than perfect and changeless; He was also omnipotent, and His unlimited power could and did produce an unlimited variety of effects.[59] Therefore Descartes considered his laws of nature as necessary but not sufficient conditions for explaining the phenomena of nature. Not only are they too broad to deal with the specific phenomena of this world exclusively, but more detailed information – empirical information – is needed if we are to know and to explain the phenomena of this world. Two factors prevent us from deriving a priori science from these general principles alone.

First, without observing, we do not know which of many possible phenomena are actually in this world. Second, any given phenomenon can be explained by several possible mechanisms, each of which is compatible with the same set of general principles. Despite the necessity of the eternal truths and the laws of nature, many aspects of the world are in fact

---

[59] Most commentators have agreed that the primary thrust of Descartes' method was deduction from first principles, however much he may have allowed for empirical factors. A few scholars, most notably Olscamp and Clerke, have pushed the opposite view to the point where they would make of Descartes a modern, hypothetico- deductivist. The view I am defending here gives ample consideration to empirical elements without losing sight of the overall structure of Cartesian thought. Errors result from giving too much weight either to Descartes' pressing philosophical goals or to his work in natural science, as if he were either a philosopher or a scientist but not both.

contingent. The particular implementation of the laws of nature in the creation is contingent. Descartes agreed that a simple effect can be explained in several possible ways, but he did not think that the possibility of things in general could be explained except in one way, which is the true one.[60] In order to know which of many possible phenomena are in the world and which of many possible mechanisms God in fact used to produce the phenomena in question, one must appeal to observation and experiment.[61]

Descartes advocated this methodological strategy in the *Discourse on Method*. If the primary thrust of Descartes' method was therefore deduction from the first causes, he did not completely ignore the evidence of the senses. Indeed Descartes undertook empirical investigations in optics and anatomy, and he incorporated empirical elements within his natural philosophy by linking them with Divine omnipotence and freedom: God's power could and did produce one universe – general structure of the world – but within this framework were an infinity of possible particulars. Thus when Descartes tried to account for the particular effects of nature, he ran hard up against the creative power of God: this concept is expressed in *The*

[60] Kenny, vol. II. p. 154. Descartes' statement here that a single phenomenon can be explained in several different ways is the hypothetical physics.

[61] James Collins, "Descartes' Philosophy of Nature," in *American Philosophical Quarterly* 5(1971): 10.

Discourse on Method:

"So many diverse ones presented themselves to me that I did not believe it possible for the human mind to distinguish between the forms or species of objects that are on the earth, and an infinity of other ones which could have been, if it had been the will of God to put them there. Nor, as a result, did I believe it possible to direct them to our use, unless it is by arriving at their causes through their effects and by using many particular experiments."[62]

If the particular effects could not be predicted from metaphysical truths, rather, then how was Descartes to know what the effects actually were? Observation and experiment would tell him. Obviously he already knew what phenomena he wished to explain; his problem was to discover them by showing that they followed from first the principles and the general effects. Descartes had reflected upon all the objects that had ever presented themselves to his senses, that is, once Descartes had determined what the actual effects were, he ventured to say that:

"I never notice a single thing about them which I could not explain quite conveniently through the principles I had discovered. But I must also confess that the power of nature is so ample and so vast, and these principles so simple and so general, that I do not see right away that it can be derived from these principles in many different ways; and my greatest difficulty is usually to discover in which of these ways the effect is derived. And to do that I know no other expedient than again to search for certain experiments which are such that their result is not the same when we explain the effect by one hypothesis, as when we explain it by another."[63]

---

[62] Oscalmp, p. 52.

[63] Ibid.

The competence of the laws of nature is such that particular effects can be derived from them in more one way, just like a problem in geometry that can be solved by different parts of reasoning, all equally correct. Observation is needed in order to determine which derivation is the right one. Descartes followed this method in the scientific treatises published in conjunction with the *Discourse on Method* as examples illustrating the power of the methods he was recommending.[64] Once experience tells us which phenomena need explaining and which explanations best conform to reality, then Descartes believed, it would be possible to deduce both the phenomena and their mechanical explanations from first principles, which embody with necessity which God endowed them at creation and which He maintains by His ordained power. Descartes did not always practice the methods that he preached.

Most of the mechanical models he described in *Le* monde and later in *The Principles of Philosophy* were highly speculative and were not grounded

---

[64] Seeking to explain the observed properties of light, Descartes elaborated three mechanical models, which enabled him to explain the phenomena of colors, the transmission of light through solid, transparent matter, and the laws of reflection and refraction. He made plausible the perception of colors by purely mechanical means by comparing it to a blind man's use of a stick to perceive the various aspects in his environment. He compared the transmission of light through solid, transparent matter to juice flowing through a vat full of grapes and passing out of a hole in the bottom of the vat. And he compared the reflection and refraction of light rays to a tennis ball, which, in the case of reflection, bounces off a hard surface, and in the case of refraction, has its motion altered in passing through a sort material, as when it strikes linen sheets or sand or mud.

in the kind of experimental practice he called for in these methodological remarks. It is worth stressing that Descartes saw the impossibility of purely a priori laws of nature all the way down to the last detail. If the general effects could be deduced from first principles alone, the particulars could not. In a letter to Mersense, Descartes revealed his dream of a priori laws of nature while confessing his inability to create it:

"For the last two or three months I have been rapt in the heavens. I have discovered their nature and the nature of the stars we see there and many other things, which a few years ago I would not even have dared to hope; and now I have become so rash as to seek the cause of the position of each fixed star. For although they seem very irregularly distributed in various places in the heavens, I do not doubt that there is a natural order among them which is regular and determinate. The discovery of this order is the key and foundation of the highest and most perfect science of material things which men can ever attain. For if we possessed it we could discover a priori all the different forms and essences of terrestrial bodies, whereas without it we have to content ourselves with guessing them a posteriori from their effects. I think that the science I describe is beyond the reach of the human mind; and yet I am so foolish that I cannot help dreaming of it though I know that this will only make me waste my time as it has already done for the last two months."[65]

Why such physics did not come to succeed? Early on, in part eight of *Regulae*, Descartes conceded that some things were beyond the reach of human knowledge, but not because of a defect in intelligence but rather due to the very nature of the problem itself, or the fact that the investigator is human. Success might depend upon a certain experiment which he is unable

---

[65] Kenny, vol. I. p. 123.

to make or it might even be that what he wants to know "wholly exceeds the power of human reason."[66] In his later works,[67] Descartes described the complexity of nature, and the creative power of God, in which he asserted that "the laws of nature we have discovered, I must also confess that the power of nature is so ample, and so vast that a given phenomena could be explained in any number of ways."[68] Of course this was only to say that his principles were vague and imprecise that they appeared to possess great fecundity from virtually any initial arrangement of particles and motions, he thought, he could deduce the present form of the world. And the objects of physics, as Descartes stated in the *First Meditation*, were 'composite', that is, they were complex and highly detailed, in contrast to the simplicity of mathematics.[69] The indeterminate nature of the particulars were attributed also to the inscrutability of God's Will; His reason alone was insufficient to determine which of the possible objects God had chosen to create.

Similarly although we could be certain that the universe consisted of one and the same matter, and that this matter was divisible into parts with

---

[66] Miller, p. 20.

[67] Starting with the sixth part of the *Discourse on Method*, and continuing through the Third and Fourth parts of the *Principles of Philosophy*.

[68] Oscalmp, p. 223.

[69] Gibson, pp. 192- 194.

essentially cyclical motions, and that motion in the world was always conserved, nevertheless, human reason was unable to determine the exact size, shapes, speeds and trajectories of these particles, for God could have arranged them in countless ways; experience alone can teach us which arrangements He actually chose.[70] As Descartes cautioned his readers in the opening paragraphs of the third part of the *Principles of Philosophy*, "we must pay attention to two things: God's infinite power and our limited reason."[71]

Hypotheses and Practical Certainty

Experiment was an essential part of Desacartes' science, since many questions could not be answered without it.[72] In order to deduce the motion of the blood, the disposition of the organs of the heart and of the parts of the body had to be known. Since Descartes lacked the required experimental evidence, he would not dare to undertake an explanation of human

---

[70] Miller, p. 106.

[71] Ibid., p. 84.

[72] Spyros Sakellariadis, "Descartes' Use of Empirical Data to Test Hypothesis," in *ISIS* 73(1982): 68 -76.

embryology.[73] Experiments were needed for the progress of human knowledge that Descartes despaired of ever having the time and the resources to complete them. In order to do all the experiments of use to him, he told Mersene, he would have to be wealthier than the kings of various nations.

The need for experiment in Descartes' physics was critical, yet its place was subordinate to the dictates of reason. As we have seen, the first principle (the laws of nature) of Cartesian physics were separated from the particulars of everyday experience by God's omnipotence and freedom. Just as there might be two clocks made by the same craftsman, Descartes argued in *Principle of Philosophy IV*, both equally good time keepers with exactly the same faces, yet constructed internally with completely different combinations of wheels; so the omnipotent God (Supreme Craftsman) could have produced all that we see in many diverse ways.[74] There was no necessary connection between the laws of nature and particular phenomena; one could not determine by reason alone which of the possible explanations was the actual explanation of a given effect. The laws of nature could be extended to the particulars only by invoking hypotheses. Since God could

---

[73] Olscamp, p. 52.

[74] http://books.mirror.org/gb.descartes.html

have arranged the shapes, sizes, and motions of particles in countless ways, we were free to make any assumptions we pleased about them, provided that the consequences agreed with experience.

Having concluded that God was free to arrange things as he had wished and not necessarily as we might have, Descartes claimed that he had done enough if those things which he had written corresponded accurately with all natural phenomena, whether or not he had found the true causes. For practical purposes, no more was required. Such things, Descartes went on to say, were 'held to be morally certain (beyond doubt), that is, to a degree which suffices for the needs of every day life; although if compared to the absolute power of God, they are uncertain.' Suppose, for example, that one were trying to read a ciphered message. If by substituting B for A, C for B, and so on, one were able to obtain a sensible message, then he would conclude that he had guessed the true pattern of the cipher, even though it is possible that the writer had actually written a different message in another cipher. Possible? Perhaps, but probable? It would "be difficult for this to happen, (especially if the message contains many words), that it does not seem credible."[75] Moreover there were things which we judge to be absolutely certain. Absolute certainty arises when we believe that it is

[75] Miller, p. 287.

wholly impossible that something should be otherwise than we judge it to be. This certainty is based on a metaphysical foundation, namely that God is in no way a deceiver, and hence that the faculty which he gave us for distinguishing truth from falsehood cannot lead us into error, so long as perceiving them distinctly. It is for this reason Descartes stated,

"Mathematical demonstrations have this kind of certainty, as does the knowledge that material things exist; and the same goes for all evident reasoning about material things. And perhaps even these results of mine will be allowed into the class of absolute certainties, (at least the principal and more general), if people consider how they have been deduced in an unbroken chain from the first and simplest principles of human knowledge. For these facts being admitted, all phenomena, at least the general features of the universe and the earth which I have described, can hardly be intelligibly explained except in the way I have suggested."[76]

As Descartes once expressed to Mersenne, "I agree that a single effect can be explained in several possible ways; but think that the possibility of things in general can be explained except in one way, which is the true one."[77] Consequently natural philosophy of Descartes consisted of the realm of absolute certainty and a priori demonstration. The general structure of the world followed from the first principles of Cartesian physics (the laws of motion, and the equivalence of matter and extension), which were revealed

[76] Miller, p. 287.

[77] Kenny, vol. II. p. 79.

to us by the light of reason and could not be otherwise, so have placed an infinity of particular things, unfettered by the necessity to choose one or another to instantiate. And the general principles by which Descartes sought to explain these contingent things were so vast and so general, that a particular phenomenon could be explained in any number of ways.

God could have chosen to employ any one of an infinite number of possible mechanisms to produce a given phenomenon. Which one he had actually chosen could be found only form experimentation. The human mind could not separate reality from possibility, actuality from contingency, without an appeal to experience. Yet even though experimentation was an integral part of the pursuit of truth, it remained subordinate to rational necessity, implemented only after one had discovered the general causes of things by pure intuition.

It is generally admitted that the laws of nature might not be completely predictable – it might dictate which effects really exist and which combinations of entities suffice to explain them – but it could never surprise us with something wholly new. For those who followed the Cartesian method, the universe was like a second-rate opera: the basic plot was known even before the curtain was raised; only the incidentals remained to be found.

Rationalism and Demonstrative Science

The essence of the biblical doctrine of creation is that God, of His own free will, gave existence to an ordered world, which continues to exist at His pleasure. By His absolute power, God freely created the eternal truths and the laws of nature, just as He freely created the other creatures. In this act of creation, God's power and freedom were absolute, unconstrained by anything else in the universe. It would therefore be heretical to hold that the laws of nature exists independently of God, even the laws of mathematics. Descartes found himself between the assertions that God's active acts are conformable to human reason and that they are wholly beyond our comprehension. His quest for epistemological foundations led him to articulate theological assumptions that bore the imprint of the medieval dialectic about the absolute and ordained power of God. But in contrast to voluntarist theology, Descartes adopted a kind of intellectualism.

Descartes believed that after God's exercise of absolute power in creating the world, He was bound by the necessity He had freely introduced into the created order. This necessity in the natural world provided Descartes with the warrant he sought for claiming certainty for scientific knowledge. Starting from God's power of transcendence, Descartes denied that any limits could be placed on God's power to create a boundless universe or eternal truths incomprehensibly different from those actually perceived by the human mind. However, because God was perfect and His Will and Intellect were one, God could not change His mind once He had chosen which truths to create. If we could gain knowledge of these truths, that knowledge would be permanent and necessary, not contingent.

As it was pointed out, Descartes held that God was entirely free at the moment of creation, but once He had freely chosen to create this particular world He was bound by His nature of immutability to refrain from intervening in the world He had created. According to Descartes, God could have created any world whatsoever. Prior to the creation, God was free to pick and choose among all of the possible worlds. Probably the clearest expression of this aspect of Descartes' philosophy was his claim that the world could have been created in such a way that two plus two three would not equal five. Because of this concept of absolute freedom, some scholars have categorized Descartes as being a theological voluntartist. This radical freedom, however, is only one aspect of Descartes' view of God's relationship to the created world. Without question, Descartes took a step away from the radical voluntarism which he based upon. Yet in and of itself this did not lead to scientific rationalism. A stable set of truths is surely a necessary condition for an a priori science of nature – if God can change His mind, then we can never be sure of our knowledge – but a sufficient condition it is not, for it provides no guarantee that we know those truths. A concern for Descartes was not whether God could have created a different set of eternal truths or even whether He could change those truths. Rather the question was whether we could in fact know the eternal truths for what they were: did the truths in our minds correspond to those in the created order? And at this point his answer was a resounding, rationalistic 'yes'.

God could not deceive us by implanting in our souls seeds of error rather than seeds of truth. It was on this bedrock of certainty that Descartes erected a demonstrative science. The limitations he placed on God's power were in keeping with the rationalist natural philosophy he had begun to construct in the *Regulae*. A fundamental problem for Descartes in the *Discourse on Method and the Principles of Philosophy* was, how to insure the certainty of human knowledge without denying the absolute freedom of God? In other words, how to reconcile the rationalist natural philosophy to which Descartes was already committed with his commitment to Divine freedom? Descartes' answer, if the foregoing analysis is correct, was to confine God's freedom to his completed creative acts. But if God's freedom is employed, His absolute power was confined to the time prior to the creation, it was not altogether denied. Initially to determine which propositions to make true and which mechanisms to place in nature remained with God's Will, not the human mind. Results of that determination were shared only partially – the eternal truths were revealed to mankind by the light of reason, but the actual mechanisms only by experience.

In spite of this unmistakable element of voluntarism, however, Descartes' ideal of science remained essentially rationalistic; the God who reigned sovereignty over the eternal truths and the laws of nature, the God who functioned as efficient cause of motion, was ultimately out of step with the scientific enterprise as Descartes conceived it. For a demonstrative science to be possible, God's absolute power had to be constrained by God's ordained power. God could not be allowed to change His decrees; the Lord of nature must not disobey His own laws by performing miraculous acts. The Sustainer of the world had to always act in the same way.

It is therefore apparent that theological voluntarism, in and of itself, need not lead to an empirical science of nature. It depends on how voluntarist notions are employed. The extreme voluntarism of Descartes' doctrine of eternal truths, as we have seen, is used only to banish all doubt from the human mind. The eternal truths, and with them, the world, could have been otherwise, but we have no way to know what they could have been, so it is pointless to inquire. And God implanted in our minds the truths that He actually did create, so we can know them with certainty. In effect, then, our minds limit the scope of God's past actions, just as His own immutability limits the scope of His present actions.

Though there is no necessary connection between voluntarist theology and empirical science, modest claims about voluntarism and early modern science should not be cast aside lightly, without further investigation. Indeed I have argued in the preceding chapters that their voluntarism was a fundamental reason why Robert Boyle and Isaac Newton rejected Descartes' version of the mechanical philosophy. I hope to have shown that theological voluntarism could be used to support a solidly rationalistic philosophy of nature. What Amos Funkenstein has written about Leibniz could be applied to Descartes: "from the source of all that he was in the Middle Ages, God became the guarantee of the absolute rationality of the world."[78]

---

[78] Funkenstein, p. 152.

Conclusion

In this chapter I have analyzed Descartes' metaphysical ideas about God that formed the foundations of his natural philosophy, in which he began with the unfettered freedom of God's Will, but then alleviated that freedom almost totally by stressing God's perfection. Perfection involves immutability, God always acted in the same way. God was entirely free at the moment of creation, but once He had freely chosen to create this particular world, God was bound by His nature, perhaps His immutability or His perfection, to refrain from intervening in the world He had created.

I have also discussed Descartes' belief that priori to the creation, God was utterly free to pick and choose among all of the possible worlds. Probably the clearest expression of this aspect of Descartes' philosophy is his claim that the world could have been created in such a way that two plus three would not equal five. A perfect God could not change His mind and could not deceive us by allowing us distinctively to perceive false propositions. Therefore the human mind became the touchstone for created reality, what the mind could not comprehend, God obviously had chosen not to create. If God was free to produce the particulars of nature in a variety of ways, He could have made only one kind of world in general, a world which conformed absolutely to the innate truths He implanted in our souls. Grounded upon such a philosophy of creation, Descartes' natural philosophy was largely a priori; the appeal to experience was required to enhance pure reason only where the vestiges of God's Will remained.

CHAPTER THREE

DIVINE WILL AND HUMAN LIMITS IN ROBERT BOYLE'S NATURAL PHILOSOPHY

CHAPTER THREE

DIVINE WILL AND HUMAN LIMITS IN ROBERT BOYLE'S NATURAL PHILOSOPHY

Introduction

Even though there were differences between science and religion, a positive connection between them is also evident. This is especially so in the natural philosophy of seventeenth century, where there was faith in a transcendent God with a belief in the value of a scientific study of the laws of nature. Pioneers in natural science asserted that God's Will and His absolute power does what He pleases and God's intellect and ordained power upholds the creation in an orderly and faithful manner. These theological interpretations of Divine attributes played a significant role in the natural science of seventeenth century.

In the previous chapter, I have discussed Descartes' rationalistic view of the laws of nature, in which he held that God had created the world according to Reason, and that human reason is capable of discerning the nature of that creation either because God implanted innate ideas about the creation or because God has created the human intellect in such a way that it might discern the necessary relations inherent in the creation.

In this chapter I look at the relation of science and religion in the thought of Robert Boyle, particularly the role of God's Will in his conception of natural philosophy. Robert Boyle saw God as the direct and free establisher of the laws of motion. These laws depended on Divine Will. He held that God, at the time of creation, was entirely free to create any world whatsoever. He also claimed that even after creation of this particular world, God remained utterly free to intervene in the world He had created. In creating the world commensurate with His infinite understanding and in limiting the rational faculties of created beings, God had deliberately left human understandings to speculate as well as they could upon the corporeal things. Thus we find Boyle defending God's sovereignty.

Boyle's Assertion on Design in Nature

Design critics often claim that the concept of design has never been useful in science. Boyle did not accept the vision of the Epicureans according to which the universe is a product of chance and therefore it makes no sense to speak of the final causes. Indeed, the working of nature shows a rationality that seems to require a superior rational cause that can account for it. For example, Boyle believed that because "God established rules of motion and the corporeal order – laws of nature," phenomena must exist to serve a certain purpose within that established order. Rather than rejecting final causes, Robert Boyle reinterpreted the notion of final cause, as a framework for natural philosophy - the idea that phenomena exist only because they have a purpose (i.e. because God wills them to be so) Accordingly, Boyle incorporated final causes into his use of the argument from design as proof of God's providential relationship to the creation and his continuing activity in the natural world. Boyle invokes final causes in scientific explanations and states that God must have created the cosmos and the laws of nature in it.

Since creation of the natural world is a contingent artifact of God, our knowledge of immutable essence must be abandoned: the attribute that exists depends solely on the Divine, which is beyond human scrutiny.[4] Boyle says that the laws of nature did not necessarily arise from the nature of matter but depended upon the Will of the Creator. They are an expression of God's Will for His creation.

---

[4] Robert Boyle, *Some Considerations Touching the Style of the Holy Scriptures*, edited by T. Birch (London: Taylor & Francis, 1965). vol. II. p. 26. Henceforth cited as "Birch."

Like other natural philosophers, Boyle presented his scientific work as the search for order in a universe regulated by an Intelligent Creator. A created universe was one in which the Creator had been free in devising the laws that nature should obey. Viewing the discovery of facts about the physical universe as a simultaneous discovery of its Creator, Boyle's conviction about both science and religion was based on fundamentals that are ultimately beyond our comprehension.

For Boyle, the religious dimension of scientific investigation was overwhelming. He considered the telescope, the microscope, the anatomical knife, and the chemical furnace as instruments of God's glory. Boyle even talked of natural philosophers as the "priests of nature" and held experimental philosophy to be the highest form of devotion to God. This positive outlook, which Boyle had to the created world rendered his scientific works meaningful and purposeful.

In spite of a common belief that mechanical philosophy would lead to atheism because explanations could be given without reference to God, Boyle argued that study of nature by experiment would lead to laws of a kind that would demonstrate the goodness, wisdom, and power of God. Things do not simply exist, they appear to have been designed for a purpose. The experimental philosophy, combined with the mathematization of the laws of nature, became the hallmark of modern science. It has been a pity that such achievements seem to have been advanced at the expense of religious commitment, a situation that would have been deplored by Boyle.

In her book *Environment and the Moral Life: Towards a New Paradigm*, Surjeet Kaur Chahal also stated as regards the Design in nature:

"We require a religious matrix which maintains man's position as an ecologically dominant being, but at the same time in no way having the permission to exploit nature. Since the earth is created by God everything has right to live, exist and flourish. For, neither have we created it nor do we have a right to destroy it. After all there is a Divine Purpose, a Divine Design behind nature."[5]

Boyle maintained that God's purposes could be discovered in nature and that searching for them made natural philosophy an important basis for recognizing God's power. This belief of his led him to argue in favor of admitting final causes in natural philosophy. For Boyle nature does embody Divine purpose, even if that purpose is unknown to us. Since the conditions in the universe which are necessary to produce the complexity that we perceive are so intricated and complex, they would not exist were there not a Designer. In his work *Final Causes of Natural Things*, wherein it is inquired, whether, and (if at all) with what cautions, a naturalist should

[5] Surjeet Kaur Chahal, *Environment and the Moral Life: Towards a New Paradigm.* (New Delhi: Ashish Publishing House, 1994), pp. 93-94.

admit them, Boyle considered finality to be imposed supernaturally by a providential God. Finality does not come from the nature of any created thing. The purpose evident in natural processes is divine purpose, imposed by God and can therefore be understood Divine purpose as efficient causes. Bolye maintained that the word 'cause' is synonymous with the word 'efficient.' We see in animals, in plants, and in other things that all parts are accommodated to certain ends. Hence, the natural world really contains only efficient causes, even if some of them express Divine purpose.

Boyle asked whether there are any knowable final causes in nature.[6] Boyle reported that he felt impelled to raise this question in reaction to two opposing schools of philosophy, which have denied that naturalists ought at all to trouble or busy themselves about final causes. The Epicureans thought that the world did not have to be created, because it was eternal, and therefore did not have a Creator. Thus there are no reasons for natural things, whether from God or nature. At the other extreme are Descartes and his followers who supposed all the ends of God in things corporeal to be sublime, and that it was presumptuous for man to think that his reason can be extended to discover them. Accepting the challenge presented by these two schools of thought, Boyle set about to answer four questions:

[6] Birch. p. 183.

1) Whether, there are any final causes of things corporeal, knowable by naturalists?

2) Whether, if the first question be resolved in the affirmative, should we consider final causes in science, or only efficient causes? In other words, should we look for purpose in things, or just describe immediate cause and effect relationships?

3) Whether, or in what sense, the acting for ends may be ascribed to an unintelligent and even inanimate body?

4) Lastly, how far, and with what cautions, arguments may be framed upon the supposition of final causes?[7]

In dealing with the first question, Boyle noted that when we speak of the ends, which nature, or rather the Creator of nature, is said to have in things corporeal, one of the following things may be signified.[8] First, in a restricted sense, there may be some grand and general ends of the whole world, such as the exercising and displaying of the Creator's immense power and admirable wisdom, for these His divine excellencies, whose productions manifest God's glory.

---

[7] Birch, pp. 349-395.

[8] F.F. Centore, "Mechanism, Teleology and Seventeenth Century Science," in *International Philosophical Quarterly* 12(1972): 553-571.

Second, there may be ends designed in the number, fabric, placing, and ways of moving the great masses of matter, for their bulks or qualities, are considerable parts of the world; since it is probable that these bodies, such as the sun, moon, fixed stars, and the earth, and perhaps the earth and the sea, were so framed and placed, as not only to be capable of preserving their own present state, but also as it was most conductive to the universal ends of the creation, and the good of the whole world,[9] Boyle called this kind of ends cosmical or systematical, regarding the symmetry of the great system of the world.

Thirdly Boyle identified what he called 'animal ends,' which are those that do more peculiarly concern the parts of animals (and probably plants too), which are those, that the particular parts of animals are destined to and for the welfare of the whole animal himself, as he is an entire and distinct system of organized parts, destined to preserve himself and propagate his species, upon such as the land, water, or air as his structure and circumstances determine him to act his part. Focusing on the question of the possibility of knowing final causes, Boyle stated that there are two ways in which man may pretend to know the ends of God in his visible works. He

[9] Roger Pilkington, *Robert Boyle: Father of Chemistry* (London: Butler Publications, 1959), p. 395.

may either pretend to know only some of God's ends, in some of his works; or he may pretend to know all his ends. It is in claiming to know all of God's ends that we act presumptuously. But to pretend to know God's ends in the former sense, is not a presumption, but rather to take notice of them is a duty. God's ends are knowable to us, a conclusion Bolye reached fporm the consideration of features of human anatomy. Citing the anatomy of the human eye, which is "exquisitely fitted to be an organ of sight," Boyle argued that there is nothing demeaning to say that we can know the ends of "an artificer, who is too intelligent either to do things by chance, or to make a curious piece of workmanship, without knowing what uses it is for, as long as we realize that our knowledge is limited. For it is not to be denied, that He may have more uses for it than one, and perhaps such uses as we cannot know. Far from demeaning God's wisdom, our claim to know final causes enhances an appreciation of His wisdom and power. Boyle stated,

"It is not injurious to the Divine Author of things, to believe that some of the ends, to which He destinated divers of his corporeal works, were to exert and communicate his exuberant goodness, and to receive from his intelligent creatures, such as men, an ardent love, a high admiration, and an obsequious gratitude, for having displayed so much wisdom and beneficence, in exquisitely qualifying his works to be wonderfully serviceable to one another, and a great number of them to be particularly subservient to the necessities and utilities of men." [10]

[10] Peter Anstey. *The Philosophy of Robert Boyle* (London: Routleg and Kegan Paul, 2000), p. 396.

We can know some of God's ends illustrates the domain of natural philosophy, which for Boyle encompassed what we would call physics as well as what we would call theology. Boyle saw no inconsistency between explaining phenomena physically, in terms of efficient causes, and at the same time understanding that they are the product of Divine purpose. If it was erroneous to say that everything in the visible world was made for the use of man, it was more erroneous to deny that any thing was made for ends investigable by man. Some purposes were clear, the manifestation of God's glory, the welfare of the creation, the welfare of individual creatures, and suitability of certain things for human needs. Boyle saw the search for mechanical structural explanations and the quest for understanding God's purpose for that design as complementary.

On the other hand, Boyle was skeptical about the probability of arriving at final causes for the physical science. He conceded that objects of the earth, like stones and metals do not infer knowledge of intention in their causes. But never did he permit such concession to eliminate the Designer. To say we cannot know all the functions that God intended for a structure does not preclude our ability to design some functions. A search for mechanical structural explanations and the quest for understanding God's purpose were required for an understanding of the laws of nature. A man might give a mechanical reason of the structure of every wheel and other parts of a watch, all the while supposing that the artificer designed it to show the hours of the day.[11] Boyle expressed,

"I see not, why the admitting, that the Author of things designed some of his works for these or those uses, amongst others, as a man may give a mechanical reason of the structure of every wheel and other part of a watch, and of their way of acting upon one another, when they are rightly put together, and, in short, of the contrivance and phenomena of the little machine; though he have that intended use in his eye, whilst he explicates the fabric and operations of the watch."[12]

In other words, although the mechanical explanations of particular phenomena can be limited to physical terms, when we appeal to the first cause of the natural world, discourse about final causes is appropriate. For instance, how is the world to be comprehended in relation to God? An explanation of impact appeals to a law of nature which, in turn, appeals to God's acts and His power. Boyle described, this essential relation of natural philosophy and theology, that

"Though I am willing to grant, that some impressions of God's wisdom are so conspicuous, that... even a superficial philosopher may thence infer, that the author of such works must be a wise agent; yet how wise an agent he has in those works expressed himself to be, none but an experimental philosopher can discover."[13]

---

[11] Steven Shapin, *Robert Boyle and the Experimental Life* (New Jersey: Princeton University Press, 1985), p. 120.

[12] M.B. Hall, Robert *Boyle on Natural Philosophy: An Essay with Selections from his Writings* (Bloomington: Indiana University Press, 1965), p. 20.

[13] Ibid., p. 30.

Design for Boyle was more than just a manifest feature of the world which pointed to a Designer. It was a necessary principle of natural philosophy, without it, the origin of the world was inexplicable. Mechanical principles alone were insufficient to account for the formation of the universe. We needed in addition power and skilful guidance of the motions of the small parts of the universal matter by the Creator.

While dealing with the second question, viz., should we consider final causes in science, or only efficient causes? in other words, should we look for purpose in things, or just describe immediate cause and effect relationships? Boyle answers that final causes are valid, but must be used with caution. He held that all considerations of final causes is not to be banished from natural philosophy; but that it is rather allowable to observe and argue from the manifest uses of things, that God pre-ordained those ends and uses. The sun, moon and other celestial bodies, excellently declare the power and wisdom, and consequently the glory of God. And from the supposed ends of inanimate bodies, whether celestial or sublunary, it is precarious to draw arguments to prove the particular nature of those bodies, or the true system of the universe. The bodies of plants and animals are so admirably designed for their functions that they were among Boyle's favorite examples of final causes in nature.[14] There is incomparably more art expressed in the structure of a dog's foot, he announced, than in that of the famous clock at Strasbourg. Nature does embody divine purpose, even if that purpose is unknown to us. Accordingly, he noted that "chance is really no natural cause or agent, but a creature of man's intellect."[15]

The concept of final causes embodied the idea that natural processes occur in order to actualize the potential form of the substance undergoing the process. Simply stated, teleology, with respect to both the human and sub-human worlds, means the predetermination of natural causes to their effects. Some objects are conscious of their destinies while others are not. Human beings can both discern many of the goals toward which subhuman entities are tending and alter many of the ends toward which they themselves tend. Hence, finality is a universal phenomenon visible throughout the whole universe. An example of these facts of nature are an acorn growing into an oak tree instead of a palm tree, a kitten growing into a cat instead of a dog, and salt dissolving in water while iron does not. A final cause does not mean that, necessarily, oak trees were designed for kittens to climb, water to

---

[14] J. McGuire, Boyle's Concept of Nature," in *Journal of History Ideas* 33(1972): 523-524.

[15] Ibid., p. 309.

dissolve salt, or the bridge of the nose to hold the eyeglasses.[16] Boyle considered finality to be imposed supernaturally by a providential God. The purpose evident in natural process is a Divine purpose, which was imposed by God himself.

Although it might be argued by some that the constantly recurring patterns of laws of nature emerged by pure chance, and chance cannot be the reason for the present sequences, since chance events by definition happen infrequently, while the course of nature is overwhelming regular and mostly predictable, we are left with two possibilities. It could be that finality is the result of natural providence which directly ordains causes to effects. In such cases all the parts of developing and interacting nature would be outer directed. Another possibility is that the acting parts of the universe are inner directed by immanent natures or powers or principles. For Boyle, nature does embody Divine purpose, even if that purpose is unknown to us. Accordingly, he noted, "chance is really no natural cause or agent, but a creature of man's intellect."[17] All things are the product of God's creation and providence, even when we are ignorant of the particular workings of that mechanism.

---

[16] McGuire, p. 109.

[17] Ibid., p. 102. Boyle fortune or chance is truly nothing in itself only the negation of foreknowledge and of the intention of the events.

With respect to the third question, whether or in what sense, the acting for ends may be ascribed to an unintelligent and even inanimate body, Boyle considered whether "unintelligent (and even inanimate)" bodies may act for ends.[18] There are two accounts on which the actions of natural agents may be said to tend to a certain end: one, when the agent has knowledge of that end, and acts with an intention to obtain it. The other is, when the action of the proximate agent is indeed so directed, as it ought to be to obtain an end, and yet that end is neither known nor intended by the proximate agent, but by a remoter agent, that is intelligent.[19] Boyle rejected the first kind of finality and declared that he meant only in the second sense. Appealing to God's wisdom in his providential creation and sustenance of the world, Boyle said,

"God was able to contrive the whole fabric, and all the parts of it, in such a manner, that, whilst his general concourse maintained the order of nature, each part of this great engine, the world, should, without either intention or knowledge, as regularly and constantly act towards the attainment of the respective ends which He designed them for, as if they themselves really understood, and industriously prosecuted, those ends."[20]

Within the framework of a mechanical account of nature, Boyle believed that it was possible to discover finality, which, like motion, was

---

[18] Shapin, p. 140.

[19] J. R. Jacob, *Robert Boyle and the English Revolution* (New York: Burtt Franklin, 1977), p. 109.

[20] Shapin, p. 80.

imposed on the matter in the world by God. The purpose evident in natural process is Divine purpose, imposed by God. Boyle inquired with what cautions final causes are to be considered by the naturalist? The cautions in question remind us of the limits of human knowledge. Boyle argued, we need to consider final causes in order to recognize God as Creator and Ruler of the universe, for without admitting final causes, we might be tempted to regard the universe as the product of blind chance.

We can certainly know many of God's ends, but God does not always reveal how a cause operates in a given instance. For example, the facts of anatomy and physiology reveal the uses to which the parts of the body were intended. Sometimes the final causes are evident that they are easier to know than the efficient causes. Thus, it is clear that the purpose of the valves in the heart is to ensure the one-way flow of blood as it circulates through the heart, but it is not at all easy to know how the valves are formed. Sometimes, from the uses of things we draw arguments, that relate to the Creator of nature, and the general ends. God supposed to have intended in things corporeal and sometimes also about the peculiar nature of the things themselves. This latter sort of arguments Boyle called purely or simply physical ones; and those of the former sort may, for distinction's sake, be stilled metaphysical ones.[21] Boyle thought that the ends of celestial bodies relate to the purposes of God in the universe. Although we can be sure that they do have ends on account of God's wisdom, it is presumptuous for us to judge of the system of the world, and of the destinations of the fixed stars so remote. Since, though it were certain, God intended they should be in some sort serviceable to us, yet He has in no way declared to us in what capacity, or to what degree, they shall be useful to us. Adding to this reminder about "the supposed destinations of celestial bodies," Boyle cautioned, "that it is yet more unsafe to ground arguments of the nature of particular bodies, that are inanimate in the world, upon the uses we think they were designed for."[22] His caution here is based on our ignorance of the particular purposes of inanimate things.

Boyle considered his sense of the limits of human knowledge to be consistent with the veneration he felt for the Creator.[23] It be here demanded, what the ends are, for which the deep and hidden parts of the stars of the firmament, were made, if they were not made for the use of man, Boyle would frankly answer, that he cannot tell: and he knows not, but such an

---

[21] Birch, p. 413.

[22] Ibid., p. 423.

[23] Ibid., p. 440.

answer may be more expressive of the profound reverence we owe the great Author of nature, than their opinion is. To say, that we do not know, why some part of a work is made by God, does both acknowledge our own ignorance, and leave it highly probable, that such pieces of work are suited to purposes worthy of Him, and suitable to them.

Despite the fact that the limitations of our knowledge prevent us from knowing the particular uses of heavenly bodies and, even, any uses of inanimate terrestrial bodies, "In the bodies of animals it is often times allowable for a naturalist, from the manifest and appropriate uses of the parts, to collect some of the particular ends, to which nature destined them. It is important to remember, however, that the ends, which we can know, are those which are for the welfare of mankind, not those which are for the usefulness of mankind. Sometimes knowledge of such ends can lead to profound understanding of both the structure and function of our body. For example, many of the facts of anatomy and physiology reveal the uses to which the parts of the body were intended. To ask how a piece of machinery worked was not to deny that each part had been designed with a function in mind. It was Boyle's contention that if William Harvey had not asked himself about the purpose of valves in the vein, he might well not have discovered the circulation of the blood. When Boyle asked Harvey what were the things, that induced him to think of a circulation of the blood? Harvey replied him that the key piece of evidence was the fact that the valves in the veins were designed in such a way that the blood can flow in only one direction.[24]

We can indeed know many of God's ends, but God does not always reveal how a cause operates in a given instance. Sometimes the causes are so evident such as the purpose of the valves of the heart, yet it is not at all an easy task to know how the valves are formed. Each creature functions in such a way as to conduce to the end of all. The study of nature then is not an end in itself. If it was erroneous to say that everything in the visible world was made for the use of man, it was more erroneous to deny that any thing was made for ends investigable by man. Uneasy by the possibility that mechanical philosophy might fall into materialism and atheism, Boyle warned against the tendency to reason from the absence of perceived ends to the absence of ends altogether. Thus he reasoned,

"I think it a duty our reason owes to its Author, to endeavour to vindicate his manifold wisdom, in this libertine age; wherein too many men, that have more wit than philosophy or piety, have, upon Epicurean (and some also even upon Cartesian) principles, laboured to depreciate the wisdom of God, and some of them presumed to censure the contrivances of these living automata, that (in their protoplasts) were originally his."[25]

---

[24] Birch, p. 24.

[25] Ibid., p. 187.

We should, instead, be aware of the limits of human understanding of God's wisdom. Since God is both a free and a most wise Agent, that He should adorn some creatures with parts or qualities that are not necessary to their welfare, but seem designed for their beauty. God may have designs about which we know nothing at all. Moreover, even though something may have been created for an end, we must be careful not to jump to conclude about the uses of things too quickly. There may be more than one use for something. We can have no certainty in such inferences. Boyle looked upon many of the arguments that others have made bold to draw from final causes, but as conjectural things.[26]

Lastly Boyle addressed the question how far, and with what cautions, arguments may be framed upon the supposition of final causes? He warned that the naturalist should not suffer the search, or the discovery of a final cause of nature's works, to make him undervalue or neglect the studious indication of their efficient causes. For, without knowledge of efficient causes, we know little of the nature of a thing. Boyle argued that the discovery of efficient causes remains the primary aim of natural philosophy, but the indication of them will not prejudice the contemplation of final causes.

---

[26] Birch, p. 184.

Boyle's Voluntarism

Central to Boyle's natural philosophy was the voluntaristic concept of God's relationship to the creation. Voluntaristic thinking insisted on God's omnipotence and His absolute freedom of Will. Nothing exists independently of Him, and nothing that He created can bind Him. Accordingly, the laws of nature are what they are because God created them. It is not the case that He created them because they are true, and God can alter them at will. The world was to God as a shadow to a man, both could be changed at will, in the twinkling of an eye.

According to Boyle's voluntaristic orientation, the laws of nature are what they are because God created them so; it is not the case that He created them because they are true; and He can alter them at will. [27] Miracles are evidence of His acting freely, since nothing, not even the laws of nature, can obstruct God from exercising His Will. God is the creator of the universe and Sustainer of the laws of nature, His ordained power is necessary to the conservation and efficacy of every particular physical agent.[28] According to occasionalist's interpretation of matter, which Boyle denied, God is working

[27] Margaret J. Osler, "Intellectual Sources of Boyle's Philosophy," in *Philosophy, Science and Religion* (Cambridge: University of Cambridge Press, 1992): 178-198.

[28] Osler, p. 180.

in every agent in such a way that no created power has any effect in things, but that God alone is the immediate cause of everything wrought. For instance, that it is not fire that gives heat, but God in the fire, and so forth.[29] But this, Boyle says, is impossible. Natural entities are incapable of sustaining the lawful order of the universe without the continued assistance of God. Boyle understood events in nature to involve immediate causal activity on the part of both God and natural entities.

Matter in Boyle's view has been endowed by God with certain powers. So matter is not completely inert. Yet even this power is imparted to it by the Divine Creator. It is not an inherent quality of matter but given to the parts of matter. It may be said, that all bodies are moved by an internal principle: as, for instance, an arrow, that actually flies in the air towards a mark, moves by some principle or other residing within itself. Boyle denied any connection between the nature of matter and the laws of nature. He explicitly says that the laws of motion did not necessarily arise from the nature of matter, but depended upon the Will of the Creator. God's ordained power is necessary to maintain the laws of motion governing the interactions of bodies. A clue bearing on the nature of this interaction is seen from his

[29] Robert Boyle, *A free Inquiry into the Vulgarly Received Notion of Nature*, ed. T. Birch (London: Taylor & Francis, 1965), p. 50.

writing,

"The quill, that a philosopher writes with, being dipped in ink, and then moved after such and such a manner upon white paper, all which are corporeal things, or their motions, may very well trace an excellent rational discourse; but the quill would never have been moved after the requisite manner upon the paper, had not its motion been guided and regulated by the understanding of the writer."[30]

Just as a pen, which is an inanimate thing, requires for its proper operation that its motion be guided and regulated by the understanding of the writer, so too, Boyle says, matter which makes up the universe, being suitably figured and moved, performs great things which it could not were it left to itself and not directed by an Intelligent Agent. Boyle stated that,

"If we consider God as the author of the universe, and the free establisher of the laws of notion, whose general concourse is necessary to the conservation and efficacy of every physical agent, we cannot but acknowledge, that, by withholding his concourse, or changing the laws of motion, which depend perfectly on his will, he may invalidate most, if not all the axioms and theorems of natural philosophy: these supposing the course of nature, and especially the established laws of motion, among the parts of the universal matter, as those upon which all the phenomena depend."[31]

The essence of Boyle's view of the manner of God's acting in the ordinary course of nature explains, for instance, God's sovereignty and His providence in the protection and rescue of the Hebrew young men

---

[30] Birch, p. 40.

[31] Ibid., p. 20.

(Shadrach, Meshach and Abednego,) from the burning furnace. Accordingly Boyle suggests that God withdraws His ordained power to the operation of the flames or suspends the fire's action. On this account God momentarily ceases to empower the fire or God endowed the Hebrew young men's bodies with special qualities which prevented the fire from having its effect on their bodies.[32]

It seemed obvious to Boyle that God not only could intervene in the world He had created, but in fact He often did. Certainly God who is powerful enough to intervene in the creation was also a God powerful enough to have created any kind of world He chose. Boyle believed that God had freely and deliberately chosen to limit the rational faculties of human beings. In creating the world commensurate with His own infinite understanding and in limiting the rational faculties of created beings, God had deliberately left human understandings to speculate as well as they could upon those corporeal, as well as other beings. Boyle's determination to limit scientific explanation to the sphere of God's ordinary activity – to what God actually did, not to what He had the power to do – betrays both a

---

[32] Boyle himself experience God's providence which also influence of his scientific outlook. God had providentially saved him from drowning at a very early age. While Boyle was a student at Eton, God had providentially saved him from being crushed when a wall in his room collapsed, as well as from being smothered by the dust caused by the collapse. In two other episodes while he was at Eton, God had, he believed, prevented his being killed in horse related accidents.

fundamental distrust of human speculation and a healthy respect for the facts as God saw fit to establish them. It is the theological roots of that attitude which I have discussed below.

Human Reason and God's Will

Some of the rationalist natural philosophers of the seventeenth century yielded to the temptation to impose the bounds of their own reason on God's absolute power, enclosing His creative acts in a box of their own thinking. However, for Boyle, the rationalist enterprise amounted to sheer, unwarranted presumption. He said that as a mortal being, we could be only incompetent judges of God's power, we cannot reach farther than our limited intellects can comprehend. The emphasis on God's Will affected not only how Boyle thought knowledge of the created world ought to be attained, but also the limits, that he believed, God had set on human reason.

Further Boyle noted the relationship of the human mind to the created world affects the ability of human beings to reason about this world. Because God created the world before He created human beings, God did not take human understanding into consideration when He created the world. Instead, God made things in such manner as He was pleased to think fit, leaving human beings to speculate about this world as best they can. Therefore God was not under obligation to conform to human notions in anything He did.

"To comprehend God's infinite nature fully required no less than an infinite understanding. Even for the corporeal works of God, our knowledge was incomparably inferior to His, for though philosophers have made ingenious attempts to explain the nature of things corporeal, yet their explications generally suppose the present framework of the world, and the laws of motion that are settled in it. But God knows particularly, both why and how the universal matter was first contrived into this universe, rather than a world of any other of the numberless constructions He could have given it; and both why those laws of motion, rather than others, were established; and how senseless matter, to whose nature motion does not at all belong, comes to be both put into motion, and qualified to transfer it according to determinate rules."[33]

Boyle criticized Descartes' rationalism as constraining God's creativity by restricting it to the capacities of human understanding. According to Descartes, just as God preserves the laws, it doesn't follow that they must be conservation laws. Nevertheless, the laws of nature, as Descartes described, have the same epistemological status as the eternal truths. They posses the same kind of necessity as the eternal truths, a necessity following from Divine immutability. Descartes' laws of nature were far from Boyle's, which God is free to alter at will. Similarly, Descartes appealed to God's immutability in justifying his conception of

---

[33] Birch, p. 50.

laws of nature. Boyle believed that the laws of nature provided the foundation from which everything in the universe as we know it can be explained. Because the laws of nature follow directly from God's immutability, they are necessarily true, and consequently we can know them in a purely rational manner. Descartes thought that God created the laws of nature to be necessary, whereas Boyle and other voluntarists did not.

Boyle considered that it is improper to argue the laws of nature which can be known in a purely rational manner. To do so was to presume too much of our own abilities, if we imagine that the omniscient God can have no other ends in the framing and governing of things corporeal, than such as we can discover. It follows that while simplicity may often be our best guide as to what working hypothesis to choose, we should not think it to be inevitably a reliable guide to truth. Reason concluded many other things which, if not directly repugnant to God's freedom, were contradicted by his works. For example, bodies of very unequal weight, if allowed to fall together, will reach the ground at the same time, that weaker sounds are transmitted through the air as swiftly as stronger ones, and that water expands rather than contracts upon freezing. Likewise reason disproved many plausible and diverse opinions, such as the blood's being conveyed from the heart by the veins (not the arteries) to the outward parts of the body, which had to be abandoned upon the discovery of phenomena with which they were inconsistent.[34]

Boyle's suspicion of pure reason was connected with his theological voluntarism. He held that further speculation on God's purposes, apart from that the Scripture reveals, was pointless, even dangerous, for it could lead us into error. Science could progress without the knowledge of ultimate realities, without encroaching on theological ground. Unlike Descartes, Boyle did not consider himself obliged to treat the cause of gravity in general in order to use it in his explanation of the cause of elasticity of air. Thus Boyle avoided the kind of rationalistic science pursued by Descartes and Cartesians. It was better to know a little with certainty from experiment than to construct speculative systems of the universe.[35] Although Boyle saw the advantage of knowing in general, how the qualities of things are deducible from matter, he affirmed that knowing merely how one body affects another was sufficient.[36] Boyle was devoted to a defense of experimentally derived knowledge in the face of contingencies. Properties,

---

[34] John H. Brooke, *Science and Religion: Some Historical Perspectives* (Cambridge: Cambridge University Press, 1998), p. 130.

[35] Brooke, p. 140.

[36] Osler, p. 100.

not essences, were the aspects of nature he sought to determine. It is no accident that among Boyle's contributions to science are his discoveries of chemical indicators and the establishment of almost all the properties of phosphorus known for centuries.

The scientists' search for mechanical explanations for nature continued with seemingly great success, but God's purposes were seen less and less by them. Boyle believed that God imposed whatever limits to understanding He thought fit, and had most likely chosen to grant greater intellects to angels than to human beings. He also believed that God, in creating the individual human beings, chose to endow some with a greater measure of intellectual abilities than others. Boyle not only believed in God's freedom to produce this natural world rather than some other, and not only in God's power to intervene in the created world, he believed that in creating the human intellect, God freely chose to limits its capacity for understanding. In Boyle's view, God, had He so chosen, could have engineered things in such a way that the human intellect would have been capable of an a priori knowledge of the natural world – but He did not choose to do so. Boyle thought that God set such limits to human understanding because he believed that God, in His infinite wisdom, has reserved in infinite understanding.

Probability and Certainty in Boyle's Voluntarism

To say that God's thoughts are higher than ours, even to stress this point as fundamental to human knowledge, is not to say that God is unfettered by any considerations whatsoever. God could have created an entirely different natural order, if it had pleased him to do so. He could not have made white snow black or hot fire cold, for such a combinations of attributes are contradictory. He could have created substances with properties different from the ones that presently exits.

There is nothing in the world that God cannot produce nothing that He cannot change, even into its opposite qualities. The inability to create contradictions lies not in a restriction to God's power but in repugnance in the things themselves because they are contradicting. To turn a sphere of silver into a sphere of gold, (in Boyle's laboratory, gold had been transmuted into a 'baser metal' with a specific gravity about two thirds of that of gold,) though difficult, was not absolutely impossible, but to make a cylindrical sphere of gold was impossible. Boyle was concerned to emphasize the power of God and inscrutability of Divine Will. Therefore Boyle distinguished between probationary truths and absolute or eternal truths.

By absolute truths, Boyle said, theoretical principles and axioms, which are the foundations of reasoning, for example, two contradictories cannot both be true. For instance every line is either straight or crooked; every number, whole and finite, is either even or odd.[37] Two quantities, that are each of them equal to the third, are themselves equal, and from truth nothing but truth can be legitimately deduced. To this sort of truths may be referred to the definitions of ideas, such as the conception we have of a triangle, a square, a circle, a cube, a cylinder, because there neither has been nor will be any time, wherein these principles of knowledge may not be assented to, without any relation to contingent circumstances. These self-evident principles may be called eternal truths.[38]

On the other hand, Boyle stated that as regards probationary truths, though man may rationally look upon them as truths, as long as he sees just cause to believe them, or no sufficient cause to question them. Knowledge, for Boyle, consists of probable statements based on our experience of phenomena. Probability is the most we can attain. He did not consider accepting probability to be a terrible compromise. Rather it is an acceptance of our own limitations. For there are doctrines and assertions that for a long

---

[37] A. Rupert Hall, *Science in Transition* (London: Williams Collin Press, 1970), p. 261.

[38] Osler, p. 134.

time generally received by philosophers themselves as truth, yet, by the discoveries of latter times, appear to unprejudiced judges to be errors. Boyle looked upon the metaphysical and mathematical principles to be truths of a transcendental kind, which does not exclusively belong to either philosophy or theology, but they are universal foundations and instruments of all the knowledge we mortals can acquire.

Thus Boyle agreed with Descartes in identifying the basic laws of mathematics and logic as eternal truths that functioned as the foundation of knowledge, including theology as well as science. Boyle affirmed that God, as the author of our reason, cannot be supposed to oblige us to believe contradiction of truth and that God's veracity and boundless knowledge prevented him from deceiving us. Here Boyle's similarity to Descartes ended. Where Descartes moved on to embraced the proposition that all things perceived clearly and distinctly were true, Boyle reminded us that we mistake and flatter human nature, when we think our faculties of understanding are unlimited, as many philosophers seems to suppose.

Boyle emphasized that we created and finite beings came into the world, as it pleases the Creator of our nature to make us. It followed from this that our mental abilities corresponded to God's designs in creating us, but may probably be supposed not to be capable of reaching to all kinds of truths, many of which may be unnecessary for us to know.[39] Thus it was not unreasonable to think that in our present mortal condition, there should be some objects beyond the comprehension of our intellects, so that we cannot attain a clear and full knowledge of them. Therefore Boyle distinguished degrees of demonstration and certainty. In metaphysical demonstration, built on the eternal truths, the conclusion was true and could not be otherwise. Physical demonstration, which presupposed physical principles (such as '*ex nihilo nihil fit*,' viz., from thing nothing comes), was less certain because it is subject to God's absolute power.

For Boyle the objective of the philosophy is not to find the certainty absolute, but the search of intelligible explanations about the mechanisms that operate underneath the phenomena, each fact contributes to the moral certainty that Boyle defines as a concurrence. Physical demonstration relied on the concurrence of probabilities, as in the agreement of testimony from two different witnesses in a murder trial.[40] It is to say a law based fundamentally on the jurisprudence, therefore, the certainty was based on the accumulated experience, but no longer it was single the experience of an

---

[39] Boyle acknowledged the human yearning for deeper knowledge of things, but he also recognized the futility of such a quest. It is not that it does not appear beautiful and desirable to know that, but that is the same manner in which it is good and desirable for us to have wings or to remain forever young.

[40] Robert Boyle. http://www.english.upenn.edu/~jlynch/Frank/People/boyle.html

individual, but of a heterogeneous group of people, the jury, where the objective era to look for the concurrence of probabilities to reach the moral certainty. The criteria of moral certainty seem to have been a product of the effort made to find criteria of evidence and test in several areas of the knowledge, from the religion to the natural philosophy, like a midpoint between certainty and opinion. Articles of religion Boyle assigned to the level of practical certainty where he also placed reasoning in physic. In many things that are looked upon as physical demonstrations, there is really but a practical certainty. For example, when astronomers discussed the paths and nature of comets, some did so without ever having seen a comet in their lives, but relied on their predecessors for information. Though the inferences they drew might have a demonstrable certainty, it was no easy task to make correct detailed and free from error observations required for constructing an undoubted theory upon them.

Boyle knew not how a number of things in physics, which men presume they believe upon strong and conviction arguments, wherein they really have but a high degree of probability.[41] In adopting this view of knowledge, Boyle rejected Descartes' view. If Descartes had admitted into natural philosophy knowledge which was not more than certainty, the

---

[41] Osler, p. 179.

propositions of his physics were derived, in his opinion, from reason alone and partook of absolute certainty. For Descartes, philosophers could learn the true structure or essence of the macroscopic and the microscopic. Whereas for Boyle, only God could have such understanding, finite men could expect no more than physical certainty. Human knowledge is not reaching with any certainty to the bottom of things, nor penetrating to their innate or inmost natures. Boyle's anti-rationalist view is that there is no necessary connection between the ideas in our minds and the external world. As Osler expressed,

"Boyle sees no necessity, that intelligibility to a human understanding should be necessary to the truth or existence of a thing, any more than that visibility to a human eye should be necessary to the existence of an atom, or of a corpuscle of air. I might here observe, that even by the same sense, some creatures may discern things, that may be perceptible to others."[42]

Atomists, Boyle observed confidently presume to know the truth and causes of the things they explicate, yet no one, Boyle thought, had shown that men must be able to explicate all nature's phenomena. How could it be proved that the omniscient God could not exhibit phenomena in ways other than those explicable by the finite reason of man? If we admit that God is the Creator of the universe, Boyle argued, how could it be that God, whose knowledge infinitely transcends ours, and who may be supposed to operate

[42] Osler, p. 198.

according to the dictates of his own immense wisdom, should, in his creating of things, have respect to the measure and ease of human understandings rather than to any other? God had made a complex world. There were often subordinate causes between particular effects and the most general causes of things. As he notices himself, since we knew very little a priori laws of nature, it was without question an advantage to have learned by a variety of experiments the differing ways, whereby nature produces the same effects. Boyle had met things, which could not be assigned a single, probable cause, and things which could be assigned several causes of widely differing character.

Boyle had often encountered such difficulties in searching into the cause and manner of things, and was so aware of his own disability to prevail those difficulties, that he dared to speak confidently and positively of few things, except matters of fact. No theory could be expected to endure all experimental tests. Boyle had seen doctrines prove conclusively wrong or false by the discovery of some new phenomena in nature, which was either unknown or not sufficiently considered, a fate which any theory could suffer if proposed too hastily.[43]

---

[43] Brooke, p. 50

The contingency of hypotheses was deep-rooted in Boyle's thought. Among the requisites of a good hypothesis was the requirement that it does not contradict any other known phenomena of nature. He who establishes a theory and expects it to last long enough to make him famous must not only take care, none of the phenomena of nature contradict his hypothesis at the present and but also the future. Boyle questioned whether philosophers realized how incomplete the history of nature was, and how difficult it was to build an accurate hypothesis, and they are subject to new findings. The future might bring new discoveries which may yet overthrow doctrines especially accommodated to the observations that have been made. The uninhabitability of the torrid zone, the solidity of the celestial orbits, and the received number of planets had all been overturned by observations.[44] Even the well-established laws of his time, the motions of the planets, Boyle was unwilling to place beyond doubt. He suspected that there may be less of accurateness, and of constant regularity, than we have been taught to believe, in the structure of the universe.[45]

---

[44] Osler, p. 30.

[45] Anstey, p. 109.

Voluntarism and Empiricism: A Manifest Connection

The goal of Boyle's scientific work, as Robert Hall has stated, was the advancement of what he was the first to call the mechanical philosophy of nature. Boyle believed that matter and motion alone could explain almost everything, except the free actions of rational agents. No other philosophy of nature, he argued, rivals the mechanical in clarity, simplicity, more than this, none other is even intelligible. For Boyle, then, the mechanical hypothesis represented the true system of the world, the correct picture of reality – at least in so far as man could discover it.

Nevertheless a hypothesis it remained, however much one may have believed in its veracity. When contrasted with the absolutely certain axioms of metaphysics, its provisional character stands out. Absolute proof is something which Boyle never claimed for the mechanical view of nature. Boyle did not want to prove that mechanical principles are the necessary and only things, whereby qualities may be explained, but that probably they will be found sufficient for their explication. It is notable that Boyle believed mechanical principles were in fact the only things whereby qualities could be explained. However, it is wholly in keeping with his conception of science that he chose to demonstrate this from the phenomena, not from any innate truths implanted in his soul.

In his critique of natural philosophy of M. B. Foster, Rolf Gruner concludes that modern science did not grow out of Christianity as an oak tree grows out an acorn. There is no necessity in the process of history, nothing natural, predestined or logical about historical development. If the preceding study of Robert Boyle has shown anything, however, it is this: within the thought of a given individual, setting aside of all questions of the flow of ideas from one person to another, a strong connection can be found between theological voluntarism and an empirical science of nature.

Boyle's attitude to the concept of natural laws derives from theological preconception. Without doubt, Boyle understood God's relation to the world in volunteristic thought. Transcendent and omniscient God was known only as He chose partially to reveal Himself in nature and in Scripture. For Boyle, it was God's power and His arbitrary Will which were paramount. God was not bound to make the best possible world or to employ, in the world He did make, notions comprehensible to merely human minds. As the product of direct Divine action, the universe reflects the laws by which God freely governed matter He had made.

Even with much aid from experience and observation, reason could go awry. Influenced perhaps by Calvinism, Boyle brought to his natural philosophy a healthy skepticism about the scope and autonomy of human reason. All hypotheses, without which there can be no science, were to a greater or lesser degree contingent on the phenomena of nature. It is therefore a voluntaristic element in Boyle's theology of creation, which impinged directly on corresponding aspects of his natural philosophy. Because the creator had worked and continued to work in accordance with His unconstrained Will and not out of necessity, the order of nature was contingent and could not be known prior to sense experience. Because the Creator had made us but mortals of limited capacity, we could not presume to share His infinite understanding of the inner constitution of things. The best that could be achieved is a hypothetical modeling of empirically determined properties, an a posteriori science of phenomena.

As Boyle said, for in the physical explanations of the parts and system of the world, it is rather like what happens when men conjecturally frame some keys to enable us to understand a letter written in ciphers. One man by his intelligence who may have found out the right key, it will be very difficult for him, either to prove otherwise than by trial, that this or that word is not such, as it is guessed to be by others, according to their keys; or to demonstrate, a priori, that theirs are to be rejected, and his to be preferred. Yet if due trial being made, the key that he proposes, shall be found so agreeable to the characters of the letter, so as to enable one to understand them, and make a coherent sense of them, its suitability is sufficient to make it accepted as the right key of that cipher.

In our attempts to interpret nature we are in a similar situation with someone who has to read an encoded letter. The meaning of the text is clear only to God; what we can do is to guess and infer a meaning which can be coherent with the context and sometimes may be true. But there are also parts of the letter which are bound to remain unclear and will probably always be like this. Moreover, both the known and the unknown can be used to testify God's Providence. Some of the unknown parts of the letter can be further clarified by God to some of us by means of grace and only because in His goodness He will decide to do so. Therefore, what we call miracles are signs of God's goodness and not events against or beyond natural order. They are miracles for us, but not for God. Such an attitude could hardly go unnoticed in the debate from which the modern philosophy of nature emerged.[46]

---

[46] Brooke, p. 40.

Gottfried Leibniz grumbled to Christiana Huygens that Boyle spends too much time, to be truthful, drawing from infinity of splendid experiments no other conclusions than those which he could have taken for principles of nature which one can certify to be true from reason alone, whereas experiments, no matter how numerous, cannot prove them.[47] It is said, by the time Huygens read Gottfried Leibniz, Boyle was dead. But ideas, like states and institutions, do not die with the individuals who shape them. Empiricism, that attitude toward nature which Boyle so strongly endorsed, and voluntarism, the theological orientation in which it thrived, both lived on in the person of Isaac Newton, one of his firmest impressionable student of Boyle's works. It is difficult to overestimate the significance of Boyle's keen sense of God's arbitrary freedom vis-à-vis even the laws of nature. Like Newton, Boyle felt no compulsion to construct a natural philosophy tied to Divine attributes and power. At the same time, both Boyle and Newton expressed man's responsibility to observe the regularities of phenomena according to experience and experiment.

Boyle's natural philosophy was more voluntaristic than that of Galileo or Descartes, precisely because he had much less confidence in fallen human minds, and placed much more emphasis on God's freedom and absolute

---

[47] Brooke, p. 67.

power. The key word here is 'emphasis.' Certainly Galileo and Descartes believed in Divine freedom and power – what many did not believe? But did they emphasize them to the extent that Boyle did? I think not. Where Galileo and Descartes reluctantly conceded that some of the things are laid beyond the power of finite minds to know, Boyle practically gloried in our status as figuratively blind and mortals, and constantly reminded us that it would be 'saucy rashness' for us to presume to bound God's freedom to make the world as he saw fit.

Conclusion

In this chapter I have discussed Boyle's belief in the incommensurability between finite created understandings and a world created in accordance with God's infinite understanding had significant implications upon his conception of the task of the natural philosopher. At the very least, we have seen that scientific knowledge was closely allied with theological propositions. Boyle determined to preserve an important role for God in his philosophy of nature. His understanding of God's relationship to the creation had important consequences for his theories of knowledge and accounts of natural world. For him, an emphasis on God's exercise of His

Will implies that when God created the human mind, He deliberately chose to limit human understanding. Human beings are capable, in Boyle's opinion, of understanding exactly as much as God intended human beings to understand, and no more.

Furthermore, Boyle's emphasis on God's Will and His absolute power means that there are no intermediaries between God and the particulars which He has created. Since God can change the order of nature at will at any time – and miracles are evidence that He sometimes does – the resulting contingency of the natural order means that human knowledge of it is restricted to what can be known through the senses. As results, the laws of nature are nothing more than empirical generalization about an observed behavior of particulars.

CHAPTER FOUR

VOLUNTARISM OF ISAAC NEWTON

CHAPTER FOUR

VOLUNTARISM OF ISAAC NEWTON

Introduction

The problem of creation, which has largely disappeared from contemporary scientific discourse, was central to the scientific revolution in seventeenth century. What modern scientists recognise as the only relevant relation man and nature was understood three centuries ago as to God's relation to the created order and His relation to created minds. For most early modern natural philosophers, both the manner in which and the degree to which the universe could be understood depended on how God had made the world, how He continued to act in sustaining it, and how He had created us. Reflection on these aspects had implications on natural philosophy.

In the preceding chapter I have discussed Boyle's conception of the laws of nature in which God's Will is evident such that no human rational process can hope to discern the features of the created world. My argument presupposes that Boyle emphasized the freedom of God's Will to create whatever world He wished and His freedom to control and dispose things as

He saw fit. God was not bound by any kind of logical necessity, nor by the laws of nature, for they were simple expression of the way He normally choose to act. The same could be said of Newton. His conception of the laws of nature reflects rather a deep commitment to the constant activity of the Divine Will.

Newton maintains that the Will of God is supreme and hence reason has to be subservient to it. Such a concept of God rejected Cartesian philosophy in favor of the belief that the properties of matter were freely determined by an omnipresent God, who remained free to move the particles of matter according to His Will. Such references to the freedom of the Divine Will were used in the seventeenth century to justify denounces on rationalist theory of nature, in which rationalists presumed to know how God must have shaped the world. Newton held that since the world is a product of God's choice rather than necessity, the laws of nature must be inferred from the phenomena of nature, not deduced from metaphysical axioms - as Descartes is accustomed to do.

Anyone familiar with Newton's life know that interest in mathematics and astronomy constituted only a part of – one may say a digression from - his main intellectual activities. His religious thought seems to have permeated his scientific writings. "It is usually considered a blemish on

Newton's life," remarked a historian, "that he spent the last twenty years working on numerology from the Scriptures, and became impatient when people asked him questions about physics."[1] As historians reported, most of Newton's intellectual efforts were not in science but in religion, chronology and alchemy. During the most productive years of his life, when he made his various discoveries, Newton devoted great time and effort to religious, historical and esoteric studies.[2]

This chapter will focus on one aspect of Newton's emphasis on God's Will and His ordained power which integrated with his natural philosophical work. I will begin with Newton's voluntaristic thinking, that is God has a continuing and active relationship with His Creation. This voluntarist conception of God as active, willful God of dominion establishes Newton's position as opposing Deism. His is neither the abstract Deity of the ancient

---

[1] Giorgio de Santillana, "The Seventeenth Century Legacy," in *Reflections on Men and Ideas* (Cambridge: Cambridge University Press, 1968), p. 179.

[2] www.newtonproject.ic.ac.uk Newton's scrutiny of nature was directed almost exclusively to the knowledge of God, as opposed to the development of new technological products. Towards the end of his life, he wrote inspiring lines that illustrate his humble recognition of the limits of his vast knowledge. "Newton, whom some say is the greatest that ever lived, invested tremendous effort in acquiring deep theological and scientific knowledge; nonetheless, he saw that all his knowledge was like a small pebble in comparison to the great ocean of truth. I don't know what I may seem to the world, but, as to myself, I seem to have been only like a boy playing on the sea shore, and diverting myself in now and then finding a smoother pebble or a prettier shell than ordinary, whilst the great ocean of truth lay all undiscovered before me."

philosophers nor the impersonal God of contemporary deists. Newton held that the laws of nature are a continuing expression of God's Will. Although committed to the mechanical philosophy, Newton was troubled by the theological implications of Cartesian mechanism. Leibniz was in the Cartesian tradition and saw God as the all-wise Creator who could make a universe that would run forever.

Newton rejected that vision, because it made God essentially unnecessary once the universe was created, and this meant that it could lead to atheism. Newton preferred a God who was always active over the laws of nature, always reminding us of His presence. In Newton, as in Boyle, one finds the defense of God's omnipresence. God works through the laws of nature, using them as His instruments. They are not self acting. Nature in her work testifies of the Intelligent presence and active agency of a Being who moves in all things according to His Will. Thus, for Newton there was no cognitive wall between the study of God and His Creation.

The Primacy of Divine Will

Divine Being has always been associated with perfection, but this has not always meant the same thing. As I have mentioned in the preceding chapters, for Galileo, a perfect God had perfect knowledge, a portion of which the human mind could share; for Descartes, perfection meant that God could not be a deceiver and had to be immutable in His actions. For Newton, God's divine perfection was tantamount with God's dominion, which he understood to be manifested in the constant activity of His Will and is the primary active force in the world. A God who had been active in the life of us also might be expected to be active in nature. Having said that God's Will is in dominion over the laws of nature and everything in the universe is nothing more than embodiment of that Will. A God without a dominion is no God at all, any more than a king without a dominion is no king.[3]

A typical picture of Isaac Newton as the model of Enlightenment deism, endorsing separation of science from religion, is a misinterpretation of the historical account of Newton's view on science and religion. He had a strong belief in the Creator, whom he referred God is PANTOKJPRATOR, the Greek word which means all powerful, almighty,[4] who holds dominion over the course of events. "The dominion or Deity of God is best demonstrated not from abstract ideas but from phenomena, by their final

---

[3] Isaac Newton, *The Mathematical Principles of Natural Philosophy,* translated by Florian Cajori (Berkeley: University of California Press, 1934), p. 544. Henceforth cited as "Cajori."

[4] Cajori, p. 940.

causes."[5] As a matter of fact, one of Isaac Newton's aims for the *Principia Mathematica* was to show that the laws of physics revealed design in the universe, which in turn evidence for a Designer. In his famous correspondence with Richard Bentley, Newton revealed this intention: "When I wrote my treatise about our system," (*The Principia*) Newton told Richard Bentley, "I had an eye upon such principles as might work with considering men for the belief of a Deity and nothing can rejoice me more than to find it useful for that purpose."[6]

Newton later added a concluding *General Scholium* and *the Principia* in which he made the argument from design explicit, proclaiming that the finely-tuned solar system could only have come from the design and dominion of an intelligent and powerful being but subject to the dominion of God. In the *Principia,* Newton answered Bentley's inquiry that could the system of the world have been produced by purely natural causes from an initial uniform distribution of matter in space? Could the planetary motions have resulted from gravitation alone, unassisted by God? The answer to both was in the negative. The only possible cause of the laws of nature and the

---

[5] Isaac Newton, *Opticks,* translated by I. Bernard Cohen (New York: Dover Publications, 1952), p. 120. Henceforth cited as "Cohen."

[6] H. S. Thayer, ed., *Newton's Philosophy of Nature: Selections from His Writings* (New York: Hafner Press, 1953), p.46.

frame of the world and the diversity of creatures was the Will of a sovereign God.[7] According to Newton gravity alone might have sufficed to give the planets their orbital speeds, but the Divine arm was required for their proper orbits around the sun. This view would lead to the belief that the laws of nature exist because God has willed them. The perfection of the laws implied for Newton a lawgiver – God, as the perfection of the architecture of the universe implied a cosmic design.

Though the orbits of the planets might continue by the mere laws of gravity, yet they could by no means have at first derived the regular position of the orbits themselves from those laws, it is not to be conceived that mere mechanical causes could cause regular orbits and motions of the planets. Such a system could only proceed from the counsel and dominion of an

[7] Like scientists of his era, Newton believed that his study of the universe ultimately revealed the glories of its Creator. Yet, Newton's goal in his masterwork "*The Mathematical Principles of Natural Philosophy*" was to explain the movements of the cosmos without using the assumption of God. The first edition of the Principia doesn't mention religion or God at all. It was only after Newton had been stung by criticisms of his materialistic approach in the Principia that he added the final "*General Scholium*" to the second edition (published in 1713), which discusses the nature of God for those readers who make it through to the end of the book. Newton's concepts of God's role in creating and maintaining the universe are revealed more in letters and other works than in the Principia. When Richard Bentley was preparing the very first Boyle Lecture, he asked Newton about evidences of intelligent design in the universe. Newton responded with four letters; the first begins with a reference to the lately published Principia, 1713 edition. By the 1710s, Newton had no difficulty discussing natural theology openly in his natural philosophical works. Even more significantly, he believed his explications of nature themselves provided powerful evidence for a Creator.

intelligent and powerful Being.[8] Moreover, Divine counsel and device were no less apparent in the animal kingdom. It could be no accident that birds, beasts, and men had a perfect symmetry of parts on both sides of their bodies, a matched pair of limbs, wings, eyes, and ears. The organs of sense and motion – above all, the eye, which Newton describes as 'truly shaped and fitted for vision' had to have been made by one who understood the nature of light, sound, and the rest of the world in which creatures had been placed. Newton, who had studied not only the nature of light but also the anatomy of the eye, continues: "did blind chance know that there was light and what was its refraction & fit the eyes of all creatures after the most curious manner to make use of it?"[9]

This compelling evidence points to the existence and dominion of God: "In the frame of animals," as Newton told William Briggs in Query 31, "God has done nothing without reason."[10] Since no reasons have been or can be assigned to a chance event, such an event would be unworthy of a rational God. If regularity pointed to choice rather than chance, variety pointed to Will rather than necessity. "Blind metaphysical necessity" (i.e. mechanical

[8] Cajori, p. 543.

[9] Cohen, p. 129.

[10] Ibid., p. 20.

action) Newton stated, "could produce no variety of things. All that diversity of natural things which we find suited to different times and places could arise from nothing but the will of a Being necessarily existing,"[11] because it is God who created all material things to set them in order.

In *Opticks*, Query 31, Newton wrote "it is unphilosophical to seek for any other origin of the world, or to pretend that it might arise out of a chaos by the mere laws of nature,"[12] and "thus much concerning God, to discourse of whom from the appearances of things, does certainly belong to natural philosophy."[13] Far from excluding teleology from natural philosophy, Newton made Divine purpose the ultimate explanation within natural philosophy. In the closing paragraph of Query 28 of the Opticks Newton stated, "the main business of natural philosophy was to argue from phenomena, and to deduce causes from effects, till we come to the very first cause, which certainly is not mechanical."[14] Thus he proposed a hierarchy of causes, each inferred from effects. Natural causes alone were insufficient to explain its regularity and variety. Newton concludes that "though every true

---

[11] Cohen, p. 546.

[12] Ibid..

[13] Ibid., p. 546.

[14] Ibid., p. 369.

step made in this philosophy brings us not immediately to the knowledge of the first cause, yet it brings us nearer to it, and on that account is to be highly valued."[15]

Similarly, in *General Scholium,* Newton expressed that natural causes alone were insufficient to explain its regularity and variety. There was only one ultimate cause of phenomena and all true science sought that cause, for true science and true religion goes hand in hand. Faith in God's dominion necessitates the belief that He is absolutely free. Newton maintains that the laws of ruling the universe do not apply to God, the First Cause. Therefore, although God had created a perfect mechanical universe, the First Cause, Newton insisted, is certainly not mechanical. To him, God appeared as "a voluntary Agent, and the uniformity of the planetary system as the effect of choice." Without doubt this world could arise from nothing but the perfectly clear free will of God directing and presiding over all. Scholars pointed out that following Robert Boyle, Newton viewed causes as divinely ordained natural phenomena that were rooted in nature by God for observers to discover through experiment.[16] Newton believed that experiment had a

---

[15] Cohen, p. 370.

[16] Two Israeli scholars have recently explored some of the implications for Newton's experimental philosophy of this belief that divine truth is implanted in nature. First, Michael Ben-Chaim has argued that Newton, following Robert Boyle, viewed causes as divinely ordained "natural capital goods" that were embedded in nature by God for

moral object, namely, to learn more about God. This is just what Newton had in mind when he expressed in *Opticks.*

"If natural philosophy in all its parts, by pursuing this method [i.e., experiment], shall at length be perfected, the bounds of moral philosophy will be also enlarged. For so far as we can know by natural philosophy what is the first Cause, what power he has over us, and what benefits we receive from him, so far our duty towards him, as well as that towards one another, will appear to us by the Light of Nature." [17]

Newton's Concept of God's Dominion

If Newton's understanding of God's dominion shaped the theological perspective in which he places his science, it also affected the actual content of his science, leading him to reject what he viewed as the materialism of both of his predecessors Rene Descartes and his contemporary Gottfried Leibniz. Neither one, as Newton saw it,[18] allowed God to exercise dominion over the laws of nature He had made.

---

observers to discover through experiment. This stance also provided a pious motivation for the study of nature. Ben-Chaim and Ayval Ramati, the two scholars show how Newton believed that experiment had a moral object, namely, to learn more about God and how to serve Him. As Ben-Chaim and Ramati observe, Newton's stated position contrasts markedly with that of Galileo, who in his Letter to the Grand Duchess Christina stressed that the study of created things that are very remote from popular understanding should be kept apart as much as possible from issues pertinent to the primary purpose of the Scripture, that is, to the worship of God and the salvation of souls. For Newton there was no such distinction.

[17] Cohen, p. 56.

[18] J.Faur, "Newton and Esoteric Knowledge", in *Cross Currents* 40 (1990): p. 527.

According to A. Rupert Hall, it was Descartes' relativistic definition of motion which first aroused Newton's opposition to Descartes' concept of the physical laws. According to Descartes, as Newton pointed out, motion is relative to contiguous bodies.[19] Since there are no bodies in the world whose relative positions remain unchanged with the passage of time, there are no fixed points of reference which enable us to locate the past position of bodies. From this, if one follows Descartes' doctrine, Newton inferred that "not even God himself could define the past position of any moving body accurately...... since in fact, due to the change positions of the bodies, the place does not exist in nature any longer."[20] Such a conception of motion was absurd to Newton, for a body could not be said to have moved from place to place. God himself could not generate motion in some bodies even though He impelled them with the greatest force. If, for example, God were to apply a great force to the starry heaven, causing it to revolve about the earth, Descartes would maintain that the earth alone and not the sky would be truly said to move, as if there were no difference between moving the

---

[19] According to Newton place is a part of space which something fills evenly. Body is that which fills place. Rest is remaining in the same place. Motion is change of place. Prior to Descartes, motion is taken to be a property of an object that is not a merely relative property. An object is either at rest or in motion, and one need not supplement assertions about the state of the object by noting that the rest or motion is being posited with respect to some reference object that one has in mind.

[20] A. Rupert Hall, *The Correspondence of Isaac* Newton (Cambridge: Cambridge University Press, 1959), p. 4.

heavens in one direction with a tremendous force and moving the earth in the opposite direction with a small force. Again, if God should cause any planets to stand still and make it continually keep the same position with respect to the fixed stars, Descartes would say that the planet moves because it is no longer at rest relative to the solar vortex of tiny material particles swinging around the sun or the orbits by a swirl, just as the same way a leaf is swirled around by a current of air, or a cork by an eddy in a stream.

Though unstated, the implication of Newton's argument was that Descartes' definition of motion placed unacceptable limits on God's ability to control His universe. The same could be said of Descartes' description of the world being of indefinite dimension. As I have mentioned in the second chapter, Descartes reserved the term 'infinite' for God alone, it is because only He could be known positively to have no limits. Other entities might have no perceivable limits and might appear to be boundless, but since we could not know positively that they were infinite, we should call them 'indefinite.' Newton did not agree. The universe is indefinite in size, he said, only before God had decreed anything about its creation – if there ever was such a time. After that time, however, the quantity of matter and the number of stars were very definitely defined. And though we were ignorant beings incapable of grasping infinity, "God at least understands that there are no limits (to space) not merely indefinitely but certainly and positively. The scope of the imaginable could not be presumed to be the same as that of God's creative act.

Newton's most voluntaristic objection to Cartesian physics was directed at Descartes' conception of matter, which Newton took for a path to atheism. The heavenly bodies exist necessarily by God's Will. Our notion of them was uncertain, because it is hardly given to us to know the limits of God's power, that is to say whether matter could be created in one way only, or whether there are several ways by which different beings similar to bodies could be produced. Newton went on to propose a thought experiment in which he appealed to God's power to create pieces of empty space containing no matter, and then to move them around as if they were pieces of matter. When Newton writes an acts of God's Will, he is not merely pointing to the fact that God could have done otherwise. And he is indicating the nature of God's act of creation as well.

Newton perceived that God creates bodies in and of space through an act of Will in the same way that we can move our bodies through an act of will. Although we do not know the mechanism whereby we accomplish this, we clearly believe that we do it. In the same way we can be assured that God creates objects in and of space, despite our inability to conceive of any mechanism whereby this is done. Thus Newton deduced a description of the corporeal nature from our faculty of moving our bodies so that God may appear (to our innermost consciousness) to have created the world solely by the act of will, just as we move our bodies by an act of will alone. So that he might show that the analogy between the Divine faculties and our own is greater than has formerly been perceived by philosophers.

The thought of this voluntaristic conception of matter, as Newton was not reluctant to say, was that "we cannot postulate bodies of this kind without at the same time supposing that God exists, and has created bodies in empty space out of nothing." On the other hand, Descartes' identification of matter and extension was manifestly "a part to atheism, both because extension is not created but has existed eternally, and so in some circumstances because we have an absolute idea of it without any relationship to God," which would make it "possible for us to conceive of extension while imagining the non-existence of God."[21] Descartes had never imagined that matter could exist, even for a moment, without the ordained power of God.

[21] Isaac Newton, "De gravitatione et Aequipondio Fluidorum," translated by A. Rupert Hall and Marie Boas Hall in *Unpublished Scientific Papers of Isaac Newton* (Cambridge: Cambridge University Press, 1962), p. 5.

As I have mentioned in the second chapter, however, God's freedom and His sovereign power were not unambiguously on the cutting edge of Descartes' natural philosophy, so Newton can readily be excused for failing to find them. Less warranted was his implicit attribution to Descartes of his own view that extension is uncreated. When coupled with Descartes' assumption that matter and extension are the same thing, the eternity of extension yields the eternity of matter, a conclusion which Descartes not only never drew but surely never believed.

A passage in the *General Scholium*, Newton argues that God is omnipresent in both space and time. The bodies God creates in space are products and indeed embodiments of His Will, the space in which they are created is not a product of His Will. Space and time are concomitants of God's existence; they simply and necessarily exist because He does. Thus all the properties of space and time are solely dependent on God's nature and are for that reason necessary properties. Space, Newton expressed in *De gravitatione*, is fundamental to the existence of every being.

"No being exists or can exist which is not related to space in some way. God is everywhere, created minds are somewhere, and body is in the space that it occupies; and whatever is neither everywhere nor anywhere does not exist. And hence it follows that space is an effect arising from the first existence of being, because when any being is postulated, space is postulated. And the same may be asserted of duration: for certainly both are dispositions of

being or attributes according to which we denominate quantitatively the presence and duration of any existing individual thing."[22]

It is therefore not surprising that the properties of such a space and time are like those attributed to God himself. Space and time are not a part of God, as has often been suggested, but are necessary consequences of His nature as a being.[23] God acts where He is, i.e., everywhere. In Him all things contained and moved. God actually and substantially exists in infinite space, He can act in and at every place. Newton also conceives God's immensity in a literal sense. In *De Gravitatione* Newton tells us a conception of Divine immensity, in which he speaks of God's 'quality of existence' as infinite with respect to absolute space.

"The quantity of the existence of God was eternal, in relation to duration, and infinite in relation to the space in which He is present. The quantity of the existence of a created thing was as great, in relation to duration, as the duration since the beginning of its existence, and in relation to the size of its presence as great as the space belong to it."[24]

So, Newton conceives the immensity of Divine existence as unlimited, for it implies that if God should fail (per impossible) to exist in

---

[22] Hall, p. 6. Newton had interpreted Genesis 1; Colossians 1:16 and Hebrews 1:2 to mean that God created time.

[23] To distinguish God from space Newton employed the Hebrew word '*makom*' to convey that God dwells in space, not that space itself is a property of God's nature. It also conveyed that the entire universe was rightly designated the temple of God.

[24] Hall, p. 6.

any particular place, His existence would be diminished, and His presence thus limited. Newton attempts to preclude this consequence by denying the possibility that a dwarf-god should fill only a tiny part of infinite space with this visible world created by Him. In Newton's mind there is a close conceptual link between Divine omnipresence and the conception of spiritual immensity. God is actually everywhere by virtue of His existence in infinite space, and in every place He wills everything that He thinks fit to choose. The immensity of God's omnipresence is manifested through His real presence in this created world and in the fact that He exists beyond it. So the quantity of existence of God is eternal in relation to duration, and infinite in relation to the space in which He is present.

As the eternal and infinite Lord of all, He governs all things and knows all things that are or can be done. He is not eternity and infinity, but eternal and infinite. The celestial bodies God creates are contingent in the sense that they are products of His Will and in every way they do not have necessary existence, but their existence as spatiotemporal entities is in no way contingent. Any world God could create would be necessarily one in space and time. Thus Newton held in God's existence there is no time in the past, present, or future at when God does not exist. Accordingly, God does not exist in timeless present, His living existence is devoid of beginning and end. He is not eternity but eternal. This view is expressed in the Principia: "since every particle of space is always, and every indivisible moment of duration is everywhere, certainly the Maker and Lord of all things cannot be never and nowhere."[25] God's relation to the frame of time and space was indeed an intimate one for Newton. In Newton's views, God's creative power is not limited to creating the present world, so long as logical impossibilities are not in question. For God cannot do what is impossible (undo what is done), any more than He can do anything that implies an imperfection (for example, lie or deceive). Given these commitments, it is not surprising that Newton claims

"God is omnipresent not virtually only, but also substantially; for power cannot subsist without substance. In him are all things contained and moved; yet neither affects the other: God suffers nothing from the motion of bodies; bodies find no resistance from the omnipresence of God. God exists necessarily and by the same necessity He exists always and everywhere."[26]

Such is Newton's conception of Divine omnipresence. For Newton, God's divine perfection was tantamount with His dominion. He also stated that the infinity of God's space is the expression of His eternal omnipresence, because God actually and substantially exists in infinite space, He can act in and at every place. He is not duration or space, but He

---

[25] Cajori, p. 545.

[26] Ibid.

endures forever, and is everywhere. Moreover, Newton believed that God not only create the world, but also He remained in dominion over the world.[27] In Him all things contained and moving might be considered of minor importance were it not for the fact that Newton's association with space with the omnipresence of God provided justification for regarding his inverse-square law of gravitation as a universal law. In Query 31 of his *Opticks,* Newton stated that because God is present in all places, He is more able by His Will to move the bodies and thereby to form and reform parts of the universe than we are to move our limbs.[28]

Influenced by Neoplatonism and his own extensive alchemical investigations, Newton rejected the mechanisms of traditional mechanical philosophies, infusing the inert world of matter with the activity of the Divine Will, either directly through the hand of God or indirectly through active principles, which gave the world a structure and order that revealed the presence of providential choice rather than blind mechanical necessity. Newton held that God control over the forces of alchemical, electrical, and vital phenomena and the cosmic force of gravitation Himself. According to

---

[27] Alexandra Koyre, "Leibniz, Newton and Clarke," in *ISIS* 52 (1961): 555-556.

[28] Cohen, p. 403. Sensorium to mean nothing more than God's presence in the world. But if God is present in the world, then it would seem, according to Leibniz, that God would have to be the soul of the world, a charge Newton himself denied in the General Scholium.

Gregory, Newton also gave God the responsibility of preventing the stars from collapsing together under the very attraction which he caused. Newton says that miracle is needed to prevent the Sun and the fixed stars from rushing together through gravity.

This is probably what Newton had in mind, which was expressed in Opticks Query 28,[29] before he agreed with Bentley that if all the matter were at first divided into several systems and every system by a Divine power were constructed like ours: yet would the outward systems descend towards the middlemost so that this frame of things could not always subsist without a Divine power to conserve it. Thus in Query 31, Newton expressed the behavior of macroscopic objects and described

"*Nature as very conformable to herself and very simple, performing all the great motions of the heavenly bodies by the attraction of gravity which intercedes those bodies, and almost all the small ones of their particles by some other attractive and repelling powers which intercede the particles.*"[30]

This is a clear expression of Newton's belief that forces act between separate particles, i.e., at a distance. In the same paragraph in Query 31, he writes,

"*The inertiae is a passive Principle by which Bodies persist in their Motion or Rest, receive Motion in proportion to the Force impressing it, and resist*

[29] Cohen, p. 369.

[30] Ibid., p. 397.

as much as they are resisted. By this Principle alone there never could have been any Motion in the World. Some other Principle was necessary for putting Bodies into Motion; and now they are in Motion, some other Principle is necessary for conserving the Motion."[31]

Newton believed that only the active intervention of God prevented both the solar system and the universe from running down. He expressed the inadequacies of a purely mechanical world. Motion is inherently subject to decay, but we find that the order in the universe is maintained by active Principles, such as are the cause of Gravity. God must have originally made particles of impenetrable matter, subjected them to these active principles. According to Newton, God had created a world containing what he labeled active principle and passive principles. Without active principles, he argued, the amount or quantity of motion in the world would decrease. These active principles were sources of activity in nature associated with matter but not inherent in it. What Newton had in mind was to distinguish between what we now call momentum and energy. Passive principles such as inertia were insufficient to account for the persistence of well-ordered motion that he observes. It is for this reason, Newton expressed,

"There is a necessity of conserving and recruiting it by active principles, such as are the cause of gravity, by which planets and comets keep their motions in their orbs, and bodies acquire great motion in falling……… And

[31] Cohen, p. 397.

if it were not for these principles the bodies of the earth, planets, comets, and sun and all things in them would grow cold and freeze and become inactive masses; and all generation, vegetation, and life would cease, and the planets and comets would not remain in their orbits."[32]

The end of Query 31, suggests a further, more cosmic sense, in which Newton believed a gravitational force directed to the center of celestial bodies was arguably insufficient to explain the origin of planetary orbits. After dismissing the view that the world could have arisen out of chaos by the mere laws of nature, Newton added in *Query 31 of the Opticks* that though being once formed, it may continue by those laws for many ages.[33] A few years before his death, Newton confided to John Conduitt what might have been the full meaning of this obscure remark.

"It was Newton's conjecture," John Conduitt pointed out, "that there was a sort of revolution in the heavenly bodies."[34] By virtue of their great masses, Jupiter and Saturn noticeably deviate in their circular bit or path and those of passing comets, which in turn deviate the rest of the planets' orbit. Vapors and light from the sun "had gathered themselves by degrees into a body and then attracted more matter from the planets,"[35] at length forming a

---

[32] Cohen, p. 399.

[33] Ibid.

[34] Ibid., p. 90

[35] Ibid., 120.

new planet and then a comet, which eventually fell into the sun and replenished its matter. The work Newton carried out with Edmund Halley in the 1680s, which determined the periodicity of comets and appears so modern, retained a supernatural role for comets, seen previously as episodic omen of doom.[36]

The God of dominion, who controls the movements of the heavenly bodies, can use comets to shape history and restore and renovate the earth. Newton expressed privately with John Conduitt, comets would eventually fall into the sun, superheating the solar sphere to such an extent that all life on earth would be burn and perish, thus necessitating the intervention of the Creator to re-populate the earth. Newton thought some day this earth would be burn and all would be perish. Apparently he believed that something like this had happened, for the earth bore visible marks of ruin upon it, which could not be affected only by deluge. When John Conduitt asked how the earth could have been re-populated if this had ever happened, Newton replied that the power of a Creator was required.[37]

According to Newton, God was not only the Being who formulated

---

[36] David Kubrin "Newton and the Cyclical Cosmos: Providence and the Mechanical Philosophy," in *Journal of the History of Ideas* 28 (1967): 325-345.

[37] R. Arthur, "Space and Relativity in Newton and Leibniz", in *British Journal for the Philosophy of Science*, (45) 1994: 219-240.

physical laws and calculated the movement of the sun and planets, He is also the one maintains that order. All systems are prone to decay and breakdown, and Newton saw that a Divine Mechanic was necessary to keep the regular order of the cosmos. This is a theme he often discussed in which the existence of God and His role in the universe. Newton's position had been described as one in which God had taken every precaution to minimize the destabilizing forces and yet had willed a world in which His intervention would also required. Newton did not see direct Divine action as a problem within his system. Quite the contrary, as I will argue below from the Leibniz - Clarke correspondence, Newton believed that God specifically intended to make a world that needed periodic protection, in order to make His governance obvious to His creatures.

<u>Newton's Voluntarism</u>

Questions about the cause of gravitation and the stability of the cosmos were fundamental to Newton's dispute with Leibniz about the nature of God's relation to the world. Newton's voluntarism, viz, the creation of the world is on God's Will, was expressed in a correspondence between Gottfried Wilhelm Leibniz and Samuel Clarke, in which Samuel Clarke was

Newton's spokesman.[38] The central issue in letters exchanged between Leibniz and Clarke was the nature of God's freedom. Is God's Will wholly conformable to His Reason? Are God's actions subject to certain rational constraints? Consistently Leibniz answered in the affirmative just as consistently Clarke answered in the negative. Gottfried Leibniz attempted to deduce facts about nature from laws he presumed to govern the Creator.

Though for Leibniz God is omnipotent there appeared to be a difficulty in describing His power as unlimited, since even God's creative power must be prescribed by logical necessity. Divine reason is prior to Divine Will such that no choice is entirely indifferent: it must be the best possible choice rationally considered. Thus God's reason in choosing to bring into existence the actual world was constrained by the laws of logic.

---

[38] When Caroline, the Princess of Wales, joined her father-in-law at court, she left behind her philosophical mentor, Gottfried W. Leibniz, with whom she continued a personal and intellectual correspondence. Her efforts to find a translator for Leibniz's *Theodicy* led her to Samuel Clarke, a disciple of Newton. Although Clarke declined to undertake the translation, he became a regular courtier and in time, an advisor to princess Caroline. When in late 1715, in answer to an inquiry about Clarke's philosophical and theological position, Leibniz sent a letter to Caroline charging Newton with theological errors, it was Clarke who took it upon himself to reply.

It is not immediately apparent that Clarke can be taken for Newton's spokesman. He was, after all, an accomplished theologian capable of debating Leibniz in his own right, and that he had been recommended as a translator for the Leibniz's Theodicy. Historians concluded that Newton worked closely with him, at least to the extent that Clarke spoke with Newton's approval. Clarke's replies reveal an intimate understanding of Newton's views on absolute space, the non-mechanical nature of gravitation, and the need for miracles in the cosmos. It was therefore assume that though Clarke likely contributed some of his own arguments to the defense of Newton's ideas, the bulk of the correspondence was written in consultation with Newton and bore his seal of approval.

On the other hand Newton denied that God must have a sufficient reason for creation, holding that He is absolutely free to create any world He so chooses by an arbitrary fiat of Divine Will, and His absolute power. Since creation is a contingent artifact of omnipotence, our knowledge of immutable essence must be abandoned: the attributes that actually exist depend solely on Divine fiat which is forever beyond human scrutiny. For Newton God is dominion continually over the laws of nature to keep creation on its course. His concept of God of dominion against Leibniz's Supramundana, whose Being is much more detached from creation. Nature is a perfect self-regulating mechanism establish by a single Divine fiat. Accordingly, there is no need for God's active intervention in the world.

Leibniz spelled out his differences with Newton in a letter to Johann Bernoulli. Newton and his followers have a very odd opinion regarding God's workmanship. According to them, God's watch - the universe - would stop working if He didn't re-wind it from time to time. Thus miracles are necessary to Newton.[39] Leibniz believed that the world needed no Divine renewal for its continued operation. In the opinion of Leibniz, Newton's concept of Divine maintenance reflected poorly on God's wisdom and power. Leibniz criticized the apparent invocation of God's intervention in

---

[39] Mordechai Feinold, "Newton and Leibniz," in *ISIS* 84 (1999): 310 - 338.

the universe that implies a defect in His workmanship. God could not be so incompetent as to create a system which was not capable of running on its own.

To this, Clarke replied that it is actually a good thing for God to be involved in the world rather than making it and walking away from it, so to speak. According to the Newton, Leibniz claimed, God had made the world imperfect that He was obliged to amend it, as a clockmaker mends his work. Clarke and Newton did not agree. The world was incapable of running on its own. God was rather himself the Creator and continual preserver of the forces in the world, so that nothing is done without His continual power and governing.[40] Clarke, a spokesman of Newton, explicitly rejects the clockwork metaphor that is so often associated with Newton's science:

"The notion of the world's being a great machine, going on without the interposition of God, as a clock continues to go without the assistance of a clockmaker, is the notion of materialism and fate, and tends, (under pretence of making God a supra-mundane intelligence), to exclude providence and God's government in reality out of the world."[41]

Both Clarke and Newton objected to Cartesian's notion of matter because it did not require a Creator, so also they objected to the Leibnizean

---

[40] McGuire, p. 305.

[41] Feingold, p. 305.

notion of the world as a machine that would run on its own. Is a perfect God who is like a watchmaker, who has built into his machine every event which he has foreordained? Or is He an omnipotent King like a king who rules his creation directly and continually as active cause of all that comes to pass? Leibniz opted for the former. Although Leibniz denied that the world is like a machine that goes on without God's interposition and strongly insisted that the things that God has created need His continual influence, he affirmed that the material world is like a watch that runs without needing to be mended by God.

In Leibniz's view, the world always contains the same amount of force and energy, which changes only by passing from one material thing to another in accordance with the laws of nature and the order that God has pre-established. And Leibniz holds that when God perform miracles, He does it not to meet the needs of nature but to meet the needs of grace. Anyone who thinks differently must have a very mean notion of the wisdom and power of God. "This opinion," Leibniz argued, "did not exclude Divine providence but made it perfect." True Divine providence requires perfect foresight - and also provision in advance for any remedies that will turn out to be needed. Otherwise God must be lacking either in the wisdom to foresee things or the power to provide for them in advance. He'll be like the God of the Socinians (fore-runners of the Unitarians), who takes each day as it comes.

Contrary to what Leibniz had argued, neither the motions of heavenly bodies nor the formation and motions of plants and animals were merely mechanical in nature. For Clarke, God's workmanship consists in its manifesting not only His power but also His wisdom. It is God's wisdom which formed at the outset the perfect and complete idea of a work that began and still carries on in conformity with that perfect idea, doing this through the continual exercise of God's power. In creation of the world, God does not make nature capable of going on without Him (like someone making a clock) because that's impossible. There are no powers of nature that are independent of God, which is why nature can't possibly continue to run without Him.

According to Newton, the wisdom of God did not consist in making the present frame of the world eternal, but only in making it to last as long as He sees fit. Nor did it consist in providing remedies for natural disorders, for with regard to God, there are no disorders, and consequently no remedies, and indeed no powers of nature at all, that can do anything of themselves. For example: the present set-up of the solar system, according to the present laws of motion, will in time fall into confusion; and after that it may be 'amended' or put into a new form. But this 'amendment' is relative to our conceptions - in performing it (if he does), God will be taking something that is confusing us, and making it easier for us to understand; He won't be taking something that has gone wrong and fixing it. In reality and from God's standpoint, the present set-up and the consequent disorder and the ensuing 'amendment' are all equally parts of the design embodied in the perfect idea that God had from the outset. Where Leibniz insisted upon limiting God's actions by the ordinary course of nature, Clarke believed that God acts in any way He like for reasons known only to Him.

It was intellectualist view that held that the existence of God's plan could be guaranteed by laws that even God must obey or by aspects of God's own nature. It was on this intellectualist basis Gottfried Leibniz attempted to deduce facts about nature from laws he presumed to govern the Creator. This works, of course, if we also assume that humans have some sort of access to these same laws - perhaps by virtue of our being made in God's image. For example, Leibniz argued against Newton that God could not make something both true and not true and that God cannot act without sufficient reason. On the other hand, God might be self-restricting. Leibniz argued that God's design must not involve corrections, which is a rationalistic view of Divine perfection, but Clarke conceived of perfection in a voluntaristic thought – perfection was whatever God had intended to do, for God is perfect.[42] Thus for Clarke and Newton, Divine wisdom was identified with dominion. God's ordained power meant His actual operation, in preserving and continuing the beings, orders and motions of all things and anything less would make Him a ruler only nominal.[43]

This Clarke's conception of Divine governance implies that the distinction between natural and supernatural is an artificial one, and of merely human convenience. He argued that natural and supernatural are nothing at all different with regard to God, but a distinction merely in our conception of things. When the sun moves across the sky every day, we call it natural; if its motion ceases for a day, we call it supernatural. But neither of these needs more power than the other, and from God's standpoint neither is more or less natural or supernatural than the other. God is present to the world, not as a part, but as a Ruler and acting upon all things. Clarke said, "He is not far from every one of us, for in Him we (and all things) live and move and have our being."[44] Even the beating of the heart, the throbbing pulse, every nerve and muscle in the living organism, is kept in order and

[42] Alexander, p. 113.

[43] Ibid., p. 26.

[44] Alexander, p. 28.

activity by the power of an ever-present God.

In his fifth reply, Clarke said that with regard to God no one possible thing is more miraculous than any other. Miracles were simply unusual acts of God, but no more or less acts of God than ordinary events of nature. The raising of a human body out of the dust of the earth we call 'a miracle;' the generation of a human body and the continual motion of the earth were 'natural, for no other reason, but because the power of God effects one usually, the other unusually. This was precisely the same view of miracles which Newton himself expressed. He wrote,

"For miracles are so called not because they are the works of God but because they happen seldom. If they should happen constantly according to certain laws impress upon the nature of things, they would no longer be wonders or miracles, but might be considered in philosophy as part of the phenomena of nature (not withstanding their being the effects of the laws impressed upon nature by the power of God) notwithstanding that the cause of their causes might be unknown to us."[45]

What Newton assumes here is that God does all things in nature, whether usual or unusual. The ones done by God's established laws tend to be usual, and we consider them natural. The ones that happen seldom, without laws, tend to arouse wonder in us and thus are termed miracles. The

[45] Cajori, p.114. It is clear that Clarke and Newton both held the highly voluntaristic interpretation of miracles, which Clarke defended in his correspondence with Leibniz.

word 'miracle' is reserved for unusual events simply because ordinary events do not create the same degree of wonder. According to Newton, miracle is a work affected in a manner unusual by the interposition of God Himself.[46]

Considering his belief about Divine activity in nature, Newton could hardly mean that miracles are not acts of God; his point can only be that they are simply extraordinary acts of God. Of course Leibniz wanted no part of this voluntarism. There is a vast difference between the natural and the supernatural, he maintained, for the latter exceeds all the powers of creatures. Leibniz offered an example, deliberately chosen to arouse the rage of Newton, the planets are swept around the sun by the vast whirlpool of subtle matter that constitutes the region of space we call the solar system. Although planets have a tendency to recede from the center of the vortex (the sun) owing to their inertia, they are held in check by the pressure of all the other matter in the universe, which is a plenum. Thus for Leibniz and other Cartesians, there is (and can be) no attraction between the sun and the planets, pulling them out of the otherwise straight path into elliptical orbits. There can be no force, there is only matter and motion, with the direct

---

[46] Peacoke Christopher F Mooney, "Theology and Science: A New Commitment to Dialogue," in *Theological Studies* 52 (1991): 289 - 329.

contact of the bodies as the only direct mechanism capable of changing motion.[47] That is why Leibniz told Clarke that the revolution of a body about a certain fixed center without any other creature acting upon it is something which could not be done without a miracle.[48] Obviously Leibniz had expressed it to draw Newton's attention.

Newton argued that gravitation had been proved by mathematical demonstrations grounded upon experiments and phenomena of nature, and Leibniz himself cannot deny this. Newton's argument showed a close link between his insistence on the reality of gravitation and his acceptance of the world created by the Will of God. Newton said, gravity should not be called a miracle just because no mechanical hypothesis had been offered to explain its operation.

"We cannot give a mechanical explanation for the hardness and inertia yet we do not call these miraculous. They are natural real reasonable manifest qualities of all bodies seated in them by the Will of God from the beginning of creation and perfectly incapable of being explained mechanically.... And therefore if any man should say that bodies attract one another by a power whose cause is unknown to us or by a power seated in the frame of nature by the Will of God,..... I know not why he should be said to introduce miracles and occult qualities and fictions into the world...... But certainly God could create planets that should move round of themselves without any other cause than gravity. For gravity without a miracle may keep the planets in."[49]

---

[47] Mooney, p. 166.

[48] Ibid., p. 300.

[49] Cajori, p. 98.

Newton spelled out precisely the fundamental disagreement with his arch rival: we cannot assume that mechanical explanation did not wholly exhaust the range of natural phenomena; the process of thought was neither mechanical nor miraculous, and the same was true of gravitation. The ontology which Newton employed recognized categories which Leibinz could only label 'occult' or 'hidden' and wish to go away. In Leibniz's *Tentamen*, Newton took exception to the hypothesis that the centrifugal tendency of a body describing a curved line in a fluid is only overcome by a contiguous moving body. Then a body is only moved by a corporeal agent and not by the human mind, unless it be corporeal, nor by God, unless He be corporeal. If so, then, God does not govern the world and so He is not the Lord God. The first cause was certainly not mechanical, if only mechanical causes could keep bodies in curved paths, then the first cause was certainly not the Lord God either. Like Leibniz, Newton called non-mechanical causes 'obscure' or 'occult'. However, unlike Leibniz, Newton asserted that they were no less real and natural. This is apparent from his letter to John Conduitt,

"Leibniz gives the name of miracles or wonders to the laws impressed by God upon nature though by reason of their constant working they create no

wonder; and that of occult qualities to qualities which are not occult but whose causes are occult though the qualities themselves be very manifest."[50]

Provided that a quality itself was not occult – that is, provided that an effect was manifest and not hidden – Newton did not hesitate to accept its reality, whether or not the cause was equally demonstrable.[51] The universe and its law were created by the Will of God, who governs the world in any manner He wishes, not necessarily as we would. God was free to impress on nature whatever laws He pleased. If God chooses to produce the gravity mechanically, then let a mechanical cause be sought. If not, the phenomenon was no less lawlike and subject to philosophical understanding. In a letter to Bentley, who was pumping him for advice on how to turn the latest science to theological advantage, Newton admitted "gravity must be caused by an Agent acting constantly according to certain laws, but whether this Agent be material or immaterial is a question I have left to the consideration of my readers."[52] The readers, including Leibniz, Newton had in mind were those

---

[50] Keith Hutchinson, "Occult Qualities in the Scientific Revolution" in *ISIS* 73(1982): 233 - 235.

[51] Newton's recognition of the limits of his vast knowledge. "I don't know what I may seem to the world, but, as to myself, I seem to have been only like a boy playing on the sea shore, and diverting myself in now and then finding a smoother pebble or a prettier shell than ordinary, whilst the great ocean of truth lay all undiscovered before me."

[52] B Cohen (ed.), *Isaac Newton's Papers & Letters on Natural Philosophy*, 2nd edition (Cambridge: Cambridge University Press, 1978), pp. 279 - 312.

of the *Principia.*

In the *Principia* Newton restrains from discussing the actual cause of gravitation, preferring instead to focus on its reality as demonstrated from phenomena. Those who vow that gravity is an occult or hidden are right, if they mean there is a certain mechanism unknown to them by which bodies fall to earth. But if any reader of Newton's *Principia* means that "this transpires without any mechanism or by a law of God which brings about this effect without using any intelligible means, then it is a senseless occult quality, which is so very occult that it can never be cleared up, even though a Spirit, not to say God himself, were endeavoring to explain it."[53] Newton could not abide by such an attitude. It was bad science and bad theology, perhaps even more the latter than the former. The implication of what Newton said is that gravity is acceptable as long as we recognize that it must have been endowed upon matter at the time of creation, since it is not logically entailed by the nature of matter, or to put it another way, it is not essential to matter. This is compatible, for example, with his statement in the *Opticks:*

"*All these things being considered, it seems probable to me, that God in the beginning formed matter in solid, massy, hard, impenetrable, moveable particles, of such sizes and figures, and with such other properties and in such proportion to space, as most conduced to the end for which He formed*

[53] Cajori, p. 668.

them.........It seems to me farther, that these particles have not only an inertiae, accompanied with such passive laws of motion as naturally result from that force, but also that they are moved by certain active Principles, such as is that of gravity, and that which causes fermentation and the cohesion of bodies."[54]

In addition, in case any body should still be in doubt about God's ability to impose gravity upon matter, it reminds us Newton later addition in the *Opticks:*

"It may be also allowed that God is able to create particles of matter of several sizes and figures, and in several proportions to space, and perhaps of different densities and forces, and thereby to vary the laws of nature, and make worlds of several sorts in several parts of the universe. At least, I see nothing of contradiction in all this."[55]

Newton's aim was to show that the laws of physics, concept of gravity revealed cosmic design in the universe - in turn evidence for a Designer. In his correspondence with Richard Bentley, Newton revealed this intention:

---

[54] Cohen, pp. 400 - 401

[55] Ibid, p. 405. Newton believed that God endowed matter with various active principles. One of these active principles was, or gave rise to, gravitational attraction. Gravity could be said, therefore, to be a property inherent in matter providing it was realized that it was a superadded property. Certainly, gravity was not to be seen as a property, which was logically entailed by the nature of matter itself. Newton's natural philosophy explained the behaviour of bodies endowed with gravitational attraction, and so reveal the regular laws, which governed gravity. What Newton freely admitted he could not do was define exactly what was the secondary cause of gravitational attraction (the primary cause was, of course, God). He could not even say whether it was material or immaterial. Part of the difficulty here was surely semantic: if matter had a property of attracting other matter at a distance without any material linkage between them, might not this property still be designated "material" by virtue of the fact that it was an epiphenomenon of matter? Be that as it may, Newton certainly never insisted that gravitational attraction must be brought about by some kind of immaterial spirit, whether divine or otherwise.

"when I wrote my treatise about our system (*The Principia*) I had an eye on such principles as might work with considering men for the belief of a Deity; and nothing can rejoice me more than to find it useful for that purpose." The diurnal rotations of the sun and planets as they could hardly arise from any cause purely mechanical, they seem to make up that harmony in solar system which was the effect of choice rather than of chance. Newton later added a concluding *General Scholium* and the *Principia* in which he made the argument from design explicit, proclaiming that "this most beautiful system of the Sun, planets and comets, could only proceed from the counsel and dominion of an intelligent and powerful being."[56]

Furthermore, at the beginning of the treatise, Newton's editor Roger Cotes expanded on the language and natural theological themes of the *Scholium* in his Preface. Cotes wrote that the *Principia* had opened up the secrets of the world, and thus "we may now more clearly behold the beauties of Nature, and entertain our selves with the delightful contemplation. In the following section I will consider more closely the relationship between Newton's voluntaristic view of God and his conception of natural philosophy.

---

[56] Cohen, p. 405. Newton could accept both views of gravity, as God's action and as a measurable, predictive phenomenon. But the latter view can guide a spacecraft to the sky, and the first view cannot.

Newton's Voluntarism and a Science of Phenomena

"Hitherto I have not been able to discover the cause of those properties of gravity from phenomena," Newton declared in the *General Scholium*.[57] Although Newton did not lack ideas about the ultimate cause of gravity, he knew that it was not mechanical. "For whatever is not deduced from the phenomena is to be called a hypothesis, and hypotheses, whether metaphysical or physical have no place in natural philosophy."[58] Newton admitted that he did not understand the nature of gravity. But he argued he could -- on the basis of his observations and experiments -- generalize about its behavior. So gravity was not mechanical, not a hypothesis. It is enough, Newton said, "gravity does really exist, and acts according to the laws and abundantly serves to account for all the motions of the celestial bodies, and from the phenomenon of the tides."[59] The essence of Newton's conception of natural philosophy was that natural phenomena could be understood adequately as phenomena, apart from any knowledge of their causes. In *Opticks* Query 31, Newton asserted, "we must learn from the phenomena of

---

[57] Cajori, p. 677.

[58] Ibid. p. 547.

[59] Ibid.

nature what bodies attract one another, and what are the laws and properties of the attraction, before we enquire the cause by which the attraction is performed."[60] Fully aware of alternatives, Newton intended his approach to be seen as the deliberate rejection of the kind of science advocated by his rivals, who sought to derive all of nature from a few principles arising from their own fertile imaginations. Even minor empirical exceptions to general rules should be investigated because they open up either the possibility of discovering interesting refinements to general rules or the possibility of formulating a more sophisticated new theory. Newton summarized his position in a letter to Roger Cotes who was supervising the publication of the second edition of the *Principia*:

"In experimental philosophy we are to look upon propositions inferred by general induction from phenomena as accurately or so very nearly true, notwithstanding any contrary hypotheses that may be imagined, till such time as other phenomena occur, by which they may either be made more accurate, or liable to exception. Hypothetical philosophy consists in imaginary explications of things and imaginary arguments for or against such explications, or against the arguments of experimental philosophers founded upon induction. The first sort of philosophy, experimental philosophy, is followed by me, the latter too much by Cartes, Leibniz and some others."[61]

---

[60] Cohen, p. 39.

[61] Cajori, p. 675.

We should treat propositions as true (or nearly true) until there are deviations that promote new research, which, in turn, lead us to refine our original propositions or reject them for new ones. That is, Newton accepts that physical inquiry may be open-ended. The above letter which Roger Cotes received made no mention of Cotes and Leibniz but Cotes did not need to be told what he could see for himself. Cotes pointed out that those who have undertaken the study of natural science can be divided into roughly three classes. [62]

First, there are those, in particular, Aristotelians, who reduce the effects of bodies to natures and specific hidden or unknown qualities, on which – they have then alleged – the operations of individual bodies depend in some unknown way. Although they affirm that individual effects arise from the specific natures of bodies, they do not tell us the causes of those natures, and therefore they tell us nothing. And since they are wholly concerned with the names of things rather than with the things themselves, they must be regarded as inventors of what might be called philosophical jargon, rather than as teachers of philosophy. The second group are the mechanical philosophers who opposed the Aristotelians. They assume

[62] Cajori, p.10.

hypotheses as first principles of their speculations, forming an ingenious romance with little resemblance to reality.

The third group is of those who profess natural philosophy. Although they too hold that the causes of all things are to be derived from the simplest possible principles [i.e., the mechanical philosophy], they assume nothing as a principle that has not yet been thoroughly proved from phenomena. They do not contrive hypotheses, nor do they admit them into natural science otherwise than as questions whose truth may be discussed. Therefore they proceed by a twofold method, analytical and synthetical. From some select phenomena they deduce by analysis the forces of nature and the more simple laws of forces, and from thence by synthesis show the constitution of the rest. This is incomparably the best way of philosophizing, which Newton justly embraced in preference to the rest. This alone is worthy of being cultivated and enriched by the expenditure of his labor.[63]

Cotes thus presents Newton with his natural philosophy as reforming and transcending the mechanical philosophy. Cotes goes on to reveal in his preface of *Principia* the religious foundation of natural philosophy, in the context of defending gravity, the third kind of group mentioned just earlier.

---

[63] Cajori, p. 20.

"Without all doubt this world, so diversified with the variety of forms and motions we find in it, could arise from nothing but the perfectly free will of God directing and presiding over all. From this fountain it is that those laws, which we call the laws of Nature, have flowed, in which there appear many traces indeed of the most wise contrivance, but not the least shadow of necessity. These therefore we must not seek from uncertain conjectures, but learn them from observations and experiments. He who is presumptuous enough to think that he can find the true principles of physics and the laws of the natural things by the force alone of his own mind, and the internal light of his reason, must either suppose that the world exists by necessity, and by the same necessity follows the laws proposed; or if the order of Nature was established by the Will of God, that himself, a miserable reptile, can tell what was fittest to be done."[64]

Or to put it another way,

"The business of true philosophy is to derive the nature of things from causes truly existent, and to inquire after those laws on which the Great Creator chose, to find this most beautiful frame of the world, not those by which he might have done the same, had he so pleased. It is reasonable enough to suppose that from several causes, somewhat differing from one another, the same effect may arise, but the true cause will be that from which it truly and actually does arise, the others have no place in true philosophy."[65]

It is admitted that Newton himself did not write this nor did he read what Cotes had written before it went to press. But Cotes said nothing which Newton had not already said in the course of his career. It was by Divine Will, not rational necessity, that matter exists and possesses the properties

[64] Cajori, p. 32.

[65] Ibid., p. 27.

that it does. Divine Will has ordered the universe and sustains it from time to time as He sees fit.

Natural laws are actively imposed by Divine Will and could differ from one part of the universe to another by varying the proportions of matter and space, and perhaps even by varying the forces, as I have been discussing in this chapter, Newton argues that "God is able to create particles of matter of sizes and figures and in several proportions to space, and perhaps of different densities and forces, and thereby to vary the laws of nature, and make worlds of several sorts in several parts of the universe."[66] Surely this is not the God of Enlightenment. I can find no necessity either in Newton's theology or in his natural philosophy, no trace of Leibniz's sufficient reason or Descartes' God of immutable decrees.

Newton's God, as Koyre has noted, was not an uninterested, an impersonal first cause. Rather He is the effective Master and Ruler of the world created by him.[67] Created – is an important word, conveying the irreducible fact that the world was not made by men. Therefore it might not be made as men would have made it. Consequently a priori knowledge of nature (priori to sense experience) could not be a science of nature at all, but

[66] Tamny, p. 403.

[67] E.A. Burtt, *The Metaphysical Foundations of Modern Physical Science* (London: Routledge and Kegan Paul, 1972), p. 135.

only a romance.[68] To Newton the public scientist we owe much of the modern understanding of nature, but to Newton the private theologian we owe no less: the attitude that what God has freely done can be learned not by inventing it, but by discovering it.

Conclusion

In this chapter I have discussed that Divine Will was also primary for Newton, who upheld God's freedom to do as he pleased both in creating the world and in sustaining it. God's omnipresence provided an explanation for the phenomenon of gravity and Newton speculated that God was the upholder of universal gravitation. Newton saw the Deity as a God of dominion who ruled creation continuously, intervening with particular providence when necessary. Here Newton's view of the providence of nature stands in stark contrast to that of Gottfried Leibniz, whose "Supramundana" used his supreme intelligence and perfect foreknowledge to set the world in motion at creation, obviating the need for intervention. The differences between these two views are pointed out in this chapter.

---

[68] Cajori, p. 10.

I have also discussed voluntarism that was central to Newton's thinking. He was devoted to establishing the reality of Divine activity in the created world. God is capable of doing anything that is not logically contradictory, that the world might have been otherwise than it is, because its creation was the voluntary act of an omnipotent God. Although God created the laws of nature, He is not bound by them. Newton believed in an all-powerful God, who once had created and still preserved this universe of matter in motion.

For Newton, a mechanical philosophy without God was unimaginable. A universe of blindly moving atoms could never accidentally produce an orderly world such as ours. Even if it could, that world would rapidly grind to a halt. A God of wisdom was necessary to create it, and a God of providence was necessary to maintain it. God chose to make a universe that ran on mechanical principles, was interesting, because it was a system of nature that humans could understand. However, our understanding is unimportant unless it leads us to continual awareness of the universe as a product of God's handiwork.

CHAPTER FIVE

CONCLUSION

CHAPTER FIVE

CONCLUSION

I began this thesis by posing a general question: what was the relation of religion to science in the seventeenth century? Drawing on the insights of Michel Beresford Foster and his followers, I narrowed the scope of my inquiry to a specific question in intellectual history: was there any relation between theology and science?

My conclusion is that theological presuppositions were closely allied with conceptions of scientific knowledge. Specifically, rationalistic theology of creation was closely linked with rationalist science, and voluntarist theology of creation was closely linked with empirical science. Based on this, I argued that an emphasis on God's Will and an ordained power of God in nature goes hand in hand with a belief that the created world is utterly contingent on His Will and that human beings can attain knowledge of what kind of world God had created only by investigating the world empirically. Whereas a de-emphasis on God's Will and His ordained power tended to hold that God had created the world according to reason, and that the world embodies at least some necessary relations. We are capable of discerning the nature of that creation by the faculty of reason, either because God implanted innate ideas about the creation or because He capable of discerning the nature of that creation by the faculty of reason, either because God implanted innate ideas about the creation or because He had created the human intellect in such a way that it might discern the necessary relationships inherent in the creation.

In the first chapter, I begin with examining Galileo's rationalistic approaches to nature, which was the consequence of his emphasis on God's Reason. It may be noted that Galileo ascribed to the Aristotelian understanding of science, according to which scientific knowledge meant fully certain and immutable knowledge. According to him, there is a limit to a natural philosopher's quest of discovering the ultimate causes. Only mathematics could provide this certainty about the ultimate causes. It was the only way in which we ascribe nature. For Galileo, science was true and necessary knowledge of nature, just as mathematics was true and necessary demonstration. Natural truths must follow necessarily in such a way that it would no middle ground between truth and falsify in physical things, so in rigorous proofs one must either establish his point beyond any doubt or else beg the question. Galileo did place limits upon human ability to fathom the depths of nature that the failure of human ability to fathom the depth of nature was not due to the exercise of an inscrutable Divine Will, but due to our finite capabilities.

It is blasphemous to suppose that the world is mathematically constructed and that man could fully comprehend its mathematical principles, for this would make man's knowledge equal to the Divine. Galileo indeed declared boldly that while man knows only a few of the mathematical truths perceived by God, his understanding of these few truth equals the Divine in objective certainty, for it succeeds in understanding necessity, beyond which there can be no greater sureness. This certainty was inborn – by means of the thought experiment, one discovered the truth which was already present in his own mind, presumably it had been implanted there by God, who has endowed us with reason and intellect.

In respect to this I have discussed Galileo's scriptural interpretation of passages, which are often quoted by the opponents of heliocentric philosophy. Galileo admitted that at first appearance there were contradictions between the Copernican and the biblical views, since several scriptural passages seemed to go against a stationary sun and a mobile earth. But he pointed out that the contradiction arose because of the literal interpretation of such passages.

In the second chapter, I have discussed that like Galileo, Descartes also held a rationalistic view of creation and the laws of nature. In emphasizing God's transcendental power, Descartes denied that any limits could be placed on God's reason and power to create a boundless universe or mathematical truths incomprehensibly different from those that the human mind perceived as necessary, e.g. he refused to deny that God could make mountains without valleys, or make the sum of one and two not equal to three.

According to Descartes, for a demonstrative science of nature to be possible, God's absolute power had to be constrained by His ordained power. God could not be allowed to change His decrees; the Lord of nature must not disobey His own laws by performing miraculous acts, the Sustainer of the world had always to act in the same way. The eternal truth and the world could have been otherwise, but we have no way to know what they could have been, so it is pointless to inquire. And God implanted in our minds the truths that He actually did create, so we can know them with certainty. In effect, then, our minds limit the scope of God's past actions, just as His own immutability limits the scope of His present actions.

We also find that Descartes stressed the unfettered freedom of God's Will, but then mitigated that freedom almost totally by stressing His perfection. Because perfection entailed immutability, God always acted in the same way. A perfect God could not change His mind and could not deceive us by allowing us distinctly to perceive false propositions, e.g. two plus two is equal to five. Thus the human mind became the touchstone for created reality; what it could not comprehend God obviously had chosen not to create. If God was free to produce the particulars of nature in a variety of ways, He could have made only one kind of world in general, a world which conformed absolutely to the innate truths He implanted in us. Grounded upon such a theology of creation, Descartes' natural philosophy was largely an a priori approach to knowledge of nature. The appeal to experience was required to increase pure reason only where the vestiges of God's Will remained.

In the third chapter, I have examined Boyle's view, which expresses when God created our mind, He deliberately chose to limit human understanding. Boyle agreed with Descartes in identifying the basic laws of mathematics and logic as eternal truths that function as the foundation of all knowledge. But where Descartes embraced the proposition that all things perceived and distinct are true- including the fundamental laws of nature, which could therefore be known from pure reason, Boyle placed the foil of God's unconstraint freedom abruptly in the path of a rationalistic science. In creating the world commensurate with His power and in limiting the rational faculties of created beings, God had deliberately left human understandings to speculate they could upon those corporeal as well as other things.

Boyle never claimed, as Descartes did, that God could have made a different set of eternal truths. He never exempted God's creative activity from the law of contradiction, that is, a proposition cannot be true and false at the same time. Yet in every other respect, his theology of creation was more voluntaristic than Descartes'. Boyle believed that God had freely and deliberately chosen to limit the rational faculties of human being. When God created the world, He was not under any obligation to conform to human thoughts or wishes. Rules by which God freely regulated His own actions, the laws of nature were not necessary truths and could have been otherwise. Therefore, they had to be inferred from phenomena and treated as hypotheses, contingent truths subject to change. As mortal beings, we could know neither God nor nature from essences and innate ideas; truths about both had to be gathered from nature and scripture, in which God reveals His Will.

In the fourth chapter, I have focussed on Newton's emphasis on God's free exercise of His Will over the nature. Like his contemporary Robert Boyle, God's Will rather than Reason was primary for Newton, who upheld God's freedom to do as He pleased both in creating the world and in sustaining it. Like Boyle, Newton held a voluntaristic understanding of God's relationship to the creation. Nothing prohibited God from acting miraculously in the cosmos. The Lord of all things governs matter and motion, the laws of nature directly by His Will, in accordance with laws of His own choosing. Knowledge of nature was attained by induction from the phenomena, not by vain speculation from supposed necessary truths.

Although mathematics played a central role in Newton's natural philosophy, mathematical truth was not identical with physical truth. He made no claims for the certainty of his physics or for the identity of his mathematical concepts with physical reality. Since matter has physical properties other than those that are purely geometrical, the science of the material world cannot be known by mathematical demonstrations alone. Like Boyle, Newton probably thought of himself as an advocate of harmony between natural philosophy and theology, for he interpreted his work in natural philosophy as establishing Divine activity in the world.

Galileo and Descartes emphasized God's rationality and were inclined to accept elements of necessity in the creation as opposed to Boyle and Newton who emphasized His absolute freedom and concluded that the world is utterly contingent. Necessity found expression in the view that the laws of nature describe the essences of things and can be known by reason, while the empiricist interpretations of scientific knowledge provided a way of thinking about the contingency of the world that no longer contained essences in a Platonic or Aristotelian sense.

A question that arises here is, were these parallel emphases any more than just parallel emphases, as interesting as it may be to discover them? No single answer is likely to satisfy everyone. If one believes, as I do, that thoughtful people like those studied in my chapters tend to strive for consistency among various parts of their minds, then these parallel emphases are in and of themselves evidence that a genuine cognitive conversation between science and theology has taken place, leading toward a unified vision of reality. As Alexander Koyre pointed out, there is relationship between a philosopher's concept of God and his conception of the proper way to go about attaining knowledge of the world, God had created. Others might call for more works of the interrelation, as it were, spelling out precisely when a given thinker came to believe precisely what of God or the world for a specific reason. For them, a definitive answer would require detailed biographical studies of a sort that have not yet really been done for any of the four figures in the preceding chapters. Still others might claim that theological language is never able to do any more than to give ultimate expression to beliefs one has already formed on more purely philosophical or scientific grounds.

Andrew Dickson White and other philosophers adherents of the conflict approaches to theology and science, for example, would find it hard to admit even the possibility that theology has helped shape the modern conception of scientific knowledge. For them, theology can only retard genuine science, not inform it. The arguments in my work are not likely to convince them that a genuine dialogue has taken place; nor can I imagine what sort of account would be convincing. There remains yet those who are convinced, as Michael B. Foster was, that Christian theology caused modern science, insofar as it led early modern thinkers to go against Greek notions of science in direct response to biblical teaching about the contingency of created nature. I reject such a claim – not because I doubt that theology influenced science in this way, but because I do not accept the narrow definition of modern science that is implicit in the claim.[1]

If many natural philosophers of the seventeenth century were convinced that the Aristotelian worldview had to be replaced, they were not all equally eager to abandon the Aristotelian notion that science consists of

[1] It is correct to say that theological assumptions were closely associated with conceptions of scientific knowledge. However, to say Christian theology had actually caused the rise of modern science turns out to be as much as an oversimplification of the actual situation as the belief that conflict between science and religion is inevitable. During the scientific revolution in seventeenth century, several fundamental changes took place, each the result of a variety of factors. To give just one example, the change in the world picture from geocentrism to helicentrism certainly shows the influence of Neoplatonism on Galileo, but voluntarist theology contributed little to this central feature of the scientific revolution.

(or at least contains) necessary truths. Many of those who took this step were, like Boyle and Newton, committed to a high view of Divine freedom that was undoubtedly related to their understanding of the Bible – and this is an important historical claim that suggests a strong consonance between science and a particular form of Christian theology. But we must not be too quick to conclude that theological voluntarism was either necessary or sufficient to bring about an empirical science of nature. To say that mechanical philosophies had their origins in voluntarist theology would be going too far, but the latter undoubtedly provided a convenient metaphysics for their promotion.

The claim that religion was conducive to the advent of modern science, and specifically, that belief in Divine creation was a major presupposition in the emergence of natural science in seventeenth-century is questionable. It has been argued that we can find no significant references to God's Will and His absolute power in Galileo, without whom the scientific revolution as I understand it would not have taken place. But more modest claims about voluntarism and early modern science should not be cast aside lightly. Certainly I have argued that voluntarism was a fundamental reason why Robert Boyle and Newton rejected the Cartesian version of mechanical philosophy.[2] Leibniz was in the Cartesian tradition and saw God as the all – wise Creator who could make a universe that would run forever. Newton rejected that vision, and this mean that it could lead to atheism. Newton preferred a God who was always with us, always reminding us of His presence. For Newton, then, a For Newton, a mechanical philosophy without God was unimaginable. A universe of blindly moving atoms could never accidentally produce an orderly world such as ours, and even if it could, that world would rapidly grind to a halt. A God of wisdom was necessary to create it, and a God of providence was necessary to maintain it. God chose to make a universe that ran on mechanical principles, was interesting, because it was a system of nature that humans could understand. However, our understanding is unimportant unless it leads us to continual awareness of the universe as a product of God's handiwork.

If many natural philosophers were convinced that the Aristotelian worldview had to be replaced, they were not yet willing to abandon the

---

[2] Some may argue against this interpretation that voluntarism of Boyle and Newton 'caused' to advocate empiricism instead of conceptualism. I would say that the interpretation is depends on the sense in which the word 'cause' is employed. Even in natural science causation is an elusive concept which some would prefer to avoid. Causation in history is considerably less clear, yet historians frequently claims to be explaining the events they have recorded and almost always use language that implies causality – conjunctions like 'because' and 'since' and adverb like 'thus' and 'therefore.' I have certainly made similar claims in this thesis. Webster's Seventh New Collegiate Dictionary states that the term cause 'applies to any event, circumstance, or condition or any combination of these that brings about or helps bring about a result.' Thus I claim that voluntarism 'caused' Boyle and Newton to advocate empiricism in that it helped bring about their rejection of conceptualism and their acceptance of an alternative science of nature.

notion that science contains necessary truths. The adoption of a more modest conception of science was left to the voluntarists, for whom a necessary knowledge of nature was incompatible with God's Will and freedom.

It has been a fundamental assumption of this thesis that religion and science were inextricably intermingled during the seventeenth century scientific revolution. For too long historians have taken Galileo's encounter with the Church as suggestive of that relationship between science and religion. The analysis presented in chapter one suggests that this view is too shallow to stand scrutiny. At a much deeper level than the superficial disputes over the interpretation of scripture, religion exerted a subtle but significant influence on seventeenth century science. In subsequent years the source of that influence – the voluntaristic notion of a God who does whatever He pleases – was set aside by deists and freethinkers. But the result of that influence –an empirical attitude toward nature – was retained.

Divine freedom had a significant influence on early modern science? To the modern mind, accustomed to a radical separation of religion form almost every aspect of intellectual life, this sounds like a contradiction. But the modern world was not erected overnight by modern minds; it has emerged slowly from a world shaped by minds not quite so modern. That it still bears the marks of its history should not be surprising.

CPSIA information can be obtained
at www.ICGtesting.com
Printed in the USA
LVHW022100220522
719445LV00008B/184

9 783772 386596